A HISTORY OF MEARNS KIRK AND ITS PEOPLE

By W.J. MacGregor
and
M.C. MacGregor

Acknowledgements

This book would not have been possible without the help and assistance of a number of people some of whom invested time and effort in collating and presenting information, in proof reading and in searching through historical records and archives to establish names and places.

Elaine Marney, John Mercer, Elizabeth Harris, David Arthur, John Henderson, Gordon Wilson, Joe Kavanagh, Roderick Campbell, Marje Gillies, Sheila Goldie, Doris Watson, Lyn Black, William Black, Isobel Dawson, Jean Greig, Jessie Campbell, James Gilchrist, Rodger Baillie, Marianne MacGregor, Jane Richmond, John Hamilton, Tim Harrison, David Kidd, Mearns History Society and Ken Mitchell at Claro Print.

Published by Mearns Kirk
On the 200th anniversary of the church building in 2013

ISBN 978-0-9576742-0-2
Printed by Claro Print

Preface

In preparing for this book I am indebted to the work of W.A. Walker in 1982 *'Twelve Centuries of Christian Witness'* and others who have previously collated and presented the history of Newton Mearns as succinctly as the available sources allow. These publications are listed in the bibliography. Any errors or omissions are mine.

It was decided that in light of the expansion of Newton Mearns in the last twenty years an entirely new publication was appropriate for the Bicentennial Edition that incorporates a history of the site and that of the surrounding Mearns Parish from earliest times. The intention is to provide as comprehensive a picture of the history of Mearns Kirk and its congregation as is possible based on the surviving parish records and congregational memory.

The story contained here is of this church and its congregation from earliest times; through the turbulent years of the Reformation and Covenanters Movement to the present and should provide a worthwhile read to anyone interested in the religious and social history of the district.

Bill MacGregor
November 2012

Contents

Acknowledgements ii

Preface iii

Contents iv

Part One: Mearns Kirk - Our History v

    Chapter One: Origins of Names and Places 1

    Chapter Two: Challenges to Authority 19

    Chapter Three: The Mearns Kirk Building - Past and Present 33

    Chapter Four

        Part One: Stained Glass Windows 47

        Part Two: Ceremonial Furniture 73

    Chapter Five: Ministers of Mearns - Past and Present 87

Part Two: Mearns Kirk The People - Past and Present 111

Appendices 137

Bibliography 152

PART ONE

Mearns Kirk – Our History

Mearns Kirk circa 1900. The old School House on the right.

Around 1900. The cottages made way for the church car park.

Chapter One:

Origins of Names and Places

The Changing Name of Newton Mearns

The spelling of Newton Mearns has changed many times over the last millennium, but what has remained constant is the community that has grown and developed here over that time. The earliest known use of it was, as we shall see later in this chapter, the name of a newly organised settlement. In later years it was simply known as 'Newton', 'Neuton' or 'Mernes' or even 'Meornef' depending on who was writing the story. In the last two hundred years, the village was known as 'Newton of Mernes' and does not seem to reach the standardised name we have today until the 19th century and the coming of Tarmacadam roads and railways.

It was my intention to add any new evidence that has come to light regarding either the founding of Mearns Parish Kirk, or the founding of a settlement in the area before the time of St. Ninian or St. Kentigern - and to an extent I have succeeded. The construction of the A726 Glasgow Orbital Bypass in the early 2000's uncovered some archaeological features, believed to be an extensive palisade (a fence made of poles driven into the ground), with possibly a Long House, that stood notionally where the A726 junction for Mearns Kirk now stands[1]. During the building of the McTaggart and Mickel 'West Acres' Estate in 2002, excavations uncovered a late Bronze Age Round House[2].

The findings of the survey of the 'Titwood Palisade' makes for an interesting read as there appears to be two distinct periods of use at the site. The first period of occupation corresponds to an early historic site with occupation dates from about 3660 to 3510BC and a further more recent occupation from about 780-1030AD - both sets of dates rely on the radio carbon dating of plant materials found at the bottom of post holes at the site. I would also suggest this find is significant: given the location, it is entirely possible that this palisade may have been used by the inhabitants of the hill fort on Duncarnock Hill, or by some other residents whose dwellings have not yet been found.

Origins of Names and Places

Mearns Kirk Church is sited less than half a mile away from the Titwood Palisade; given this location and the fact that the first official records of a church on the site date back to the 12th century, there is every possibility that the church location began its life as a wayside altar dedicated to St. Bride, who was very influential in the early church and whose name appears in numerous sites in the West of Scotland (for example East "Kilbride" – the "Church of St. Bride").

So far the archaeological study of the district has been reasonably productive. Duncarnock Hill Fort has recently been excavated and a plan of it now exists on the Royal Commission for the Ancient and Historical Monuments of Scotland website, coupled with the discovery of the late Bronze Age Round House at the site of the West Acres Estate. With the inevitable expansion of Newton Mearns into the green belt I wonder what will be found next!

The images on the following pages show views from the excavations at the Titwood Palisade together with a map showing the relationship between the site and Mearns Kirk.

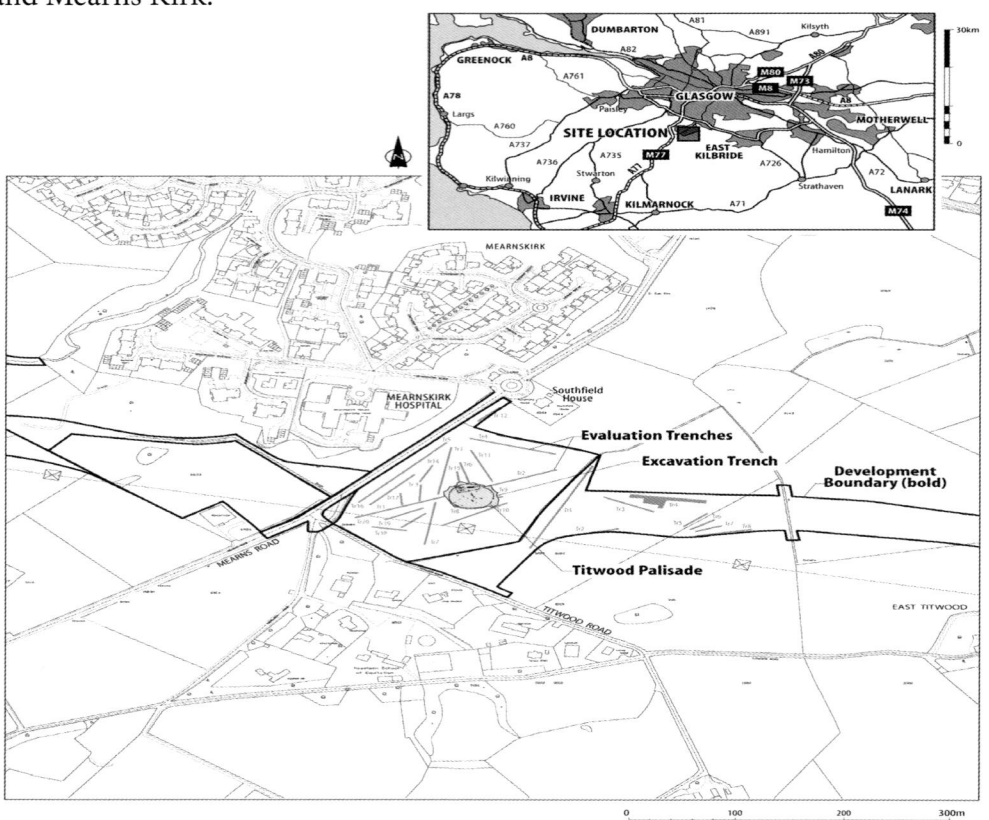

Origins of Names and Places

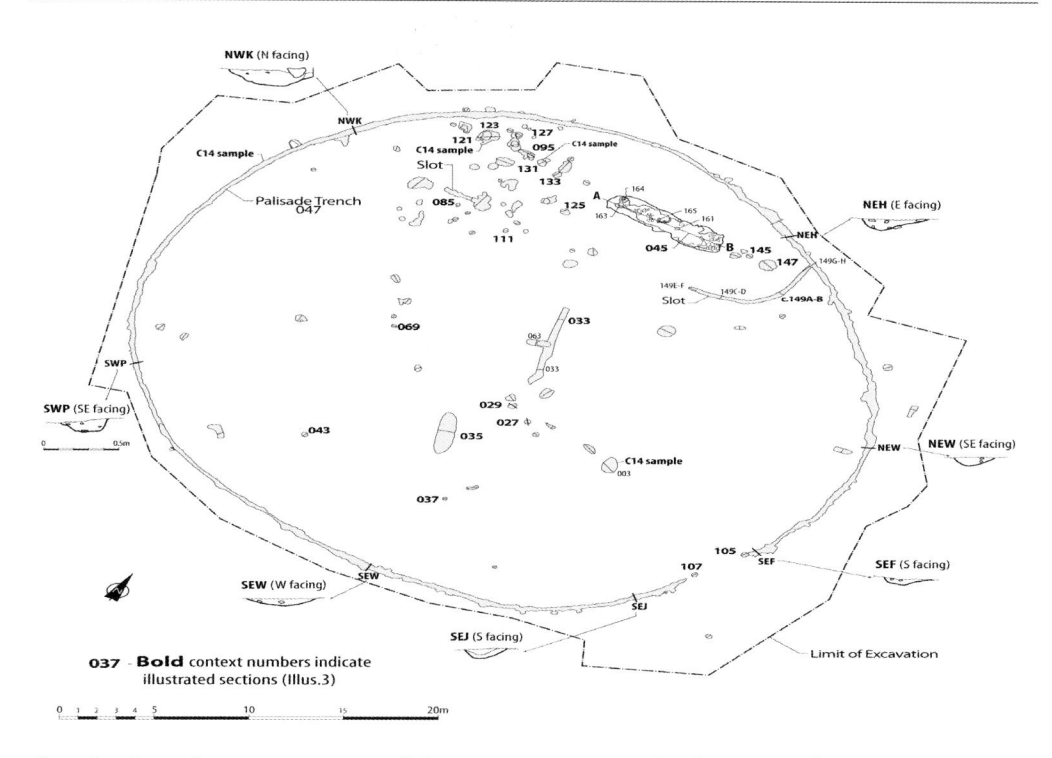

Sketch plan showing extent of the excavations with photograph

Bronze Age Land Use

The name of Mearns is ancient; exactly how ancient is not known, but what is known is that a settlement of hunter gatherers existed here in the late Bronze Age about 1600-1520 BC. Numerous wedge hammers and stone axes have been regularly found in the parish from as far back as the 19th century, when a large wedge shaped hammer head of greenstone was found and given to the National Museum of Antiquities of Scotland in 1887. A cup and ring marked rock was found near the railway at Capelrig, which is currently on the Rouken Glen golf course beside the old 'Dovecot'. Recent excavations in the district here have provided further examples of Bronze Age land use such as the aforementioned West Acres development on the Barrhead Road where in 2002 a Bronze Age round house was found[3], as shown on the opposite page.

The diameter of the round house is between 10-14 metres; the artist's impression of what may be happening within is shown above.

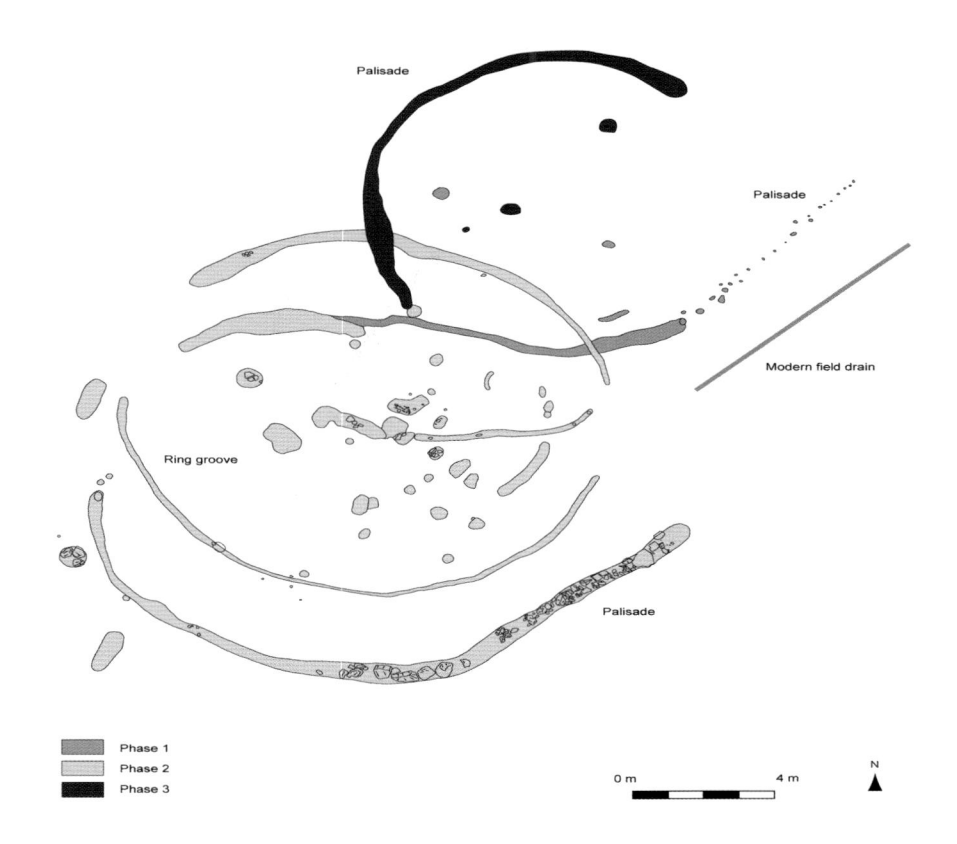

New 'Ton' Mearns or 'Villa Nova'?

There are no records of a village or town called Mearns prior to 1165, when it first appears in official records. The next record of the settlement of 'Meornes' in any official publication is in the 'Register of the Monastery at Paisley Abbey' in 1179. We also find a reference to a new town in the same records ten years or so later where we are introduced to Ronald de 'Mernes' who resided in the 'Villa Nova of 'Neuton', possibly a castle at Robshill.

The name of 'Mearns' is itself unusual and today is found in only two places in Scotland; here and Kincardineshire in North East Scotland. My research suggests that there were other instances of the name 'Mearns' being used in the middle ages in South West Scotland, particularly in the area surrounding Mauchline in Ayrshire, but these names have fallen from common use.

Origins of Names and Places

'Mearns' in whatever spelling is thought to derive from the language of the ancient Britons. According to Watson[4], the term 'Maoirne' does not appear in either Scots or Irish Gaelic, but does in Welsh Gaelic; 'Maorini' meaning 'Stewartry' or stewardship of the land. The name 'Maeronas' appears in ancient Briton and according to Crawford, the historiographer of Queen Anne, 'Mearns' means *'district of the herdsmen'*, which, given the pastoral nature of the society is a suitable one.

Perhaps a definition of the name has already been given by one of our own? The Rev. George McLatchie when writing his account of the parish for the Statistical Account of Scotland in 1792 gave a position similar to that later taken by Watson…

'[…] that the name may be a common name for any area of an indefinite extent of pastoral country which in later times took the name of kirk towns…'

It may be that "Mearns" derived from the ruling class, as Watson suggests. To help them govern in the various regions of their kingdom, local princes often appointed officers of state. One of the principal officials was the *'MAER'* who had an area allotted to him. *'An Mhaoirne'* (of which the English form is Mearns) means Stewardship. This has passed into common language and is reflected in the modern Scots Gaelic name for Newton Mearns; *Baile Ùr na Maoirne*.[5]

While we are on the subject of names of places; *'Kirk'* the Scots name for a church has always bothered me, as it seems so Anglo-Saxon. It appears, according to Nicolaisen (2001) to derive from *'Kirkja'* the Norse name for a church.[6] Given the influence of Norse culture in the West of Scotland and Ireland in the first millennium AD, I would tend to accept this argument.

The Celtic Church

Christianity was brought to Scotland by St. Ninian, who in 397 AD erected a small primitive church at Whithorn - the first stone church in Scotland. St. Columba came to Scotland in 563 AD and founded a monastery on Iona. The early churches were primitive affairs of mud and wattle, completely different from their later counterparts of sculptured stone and glass. When one was destroyed little often remained to mark the site, except perhaps only a name, but the name is the one thing that is passed down to us through the ages.

These early Christian missionaries and their disciples carried their message across the country. In St. Ninians time it was spread to the Forth and Clyde valleys and to the east coast as far north as Nairn; the Western Isles had to wait for St. Columba in the 6th Century for their conversion to Christianity.

St. Ninian also founded a Christian community at Glasgow and two centuries later St. Kentigern became the first Bishop of Glasgow. He renewed Christianity in the kingdom of Strathclyde as it had declined since the death of St. Ninian. The map on the next page shows how Scotland was divided into separate kingdoms and how Christianity spread from Ireland to the west coast of Scotland.

During the turbulent times of the Viking raids of 8th and 9th centuries, most of the monasteries and churches in Scotland were destroyed and Christianity almost disappeared. Burleigh, in his history of the Church of Scotland, suggests that the decline in Christianity between the 5th century and the 9th century was due to the predations of the Vikings and the almost continuous feuding between the various Scots kingdoms during this period. This state of affairs remained until Kenneth McAlpin seized the thrones of the smaller Scottish kingdoms and unified them into the Kingdom of Alba, with himself as king. Kenneth was finally able to fend off the invasions of the Vikings, for whom the plunder of a Christian community was especially attractive in monetary terms, but did lasting damage to organised religion.

What we now call the central belt of Scotland had been converted to Christianity by the 5th century AD. St. Patrick provides us with a record of this by describing the Picts in his letter to Coroticus in 461 AD as 'apostate'.[7]

Origins of Names and Places

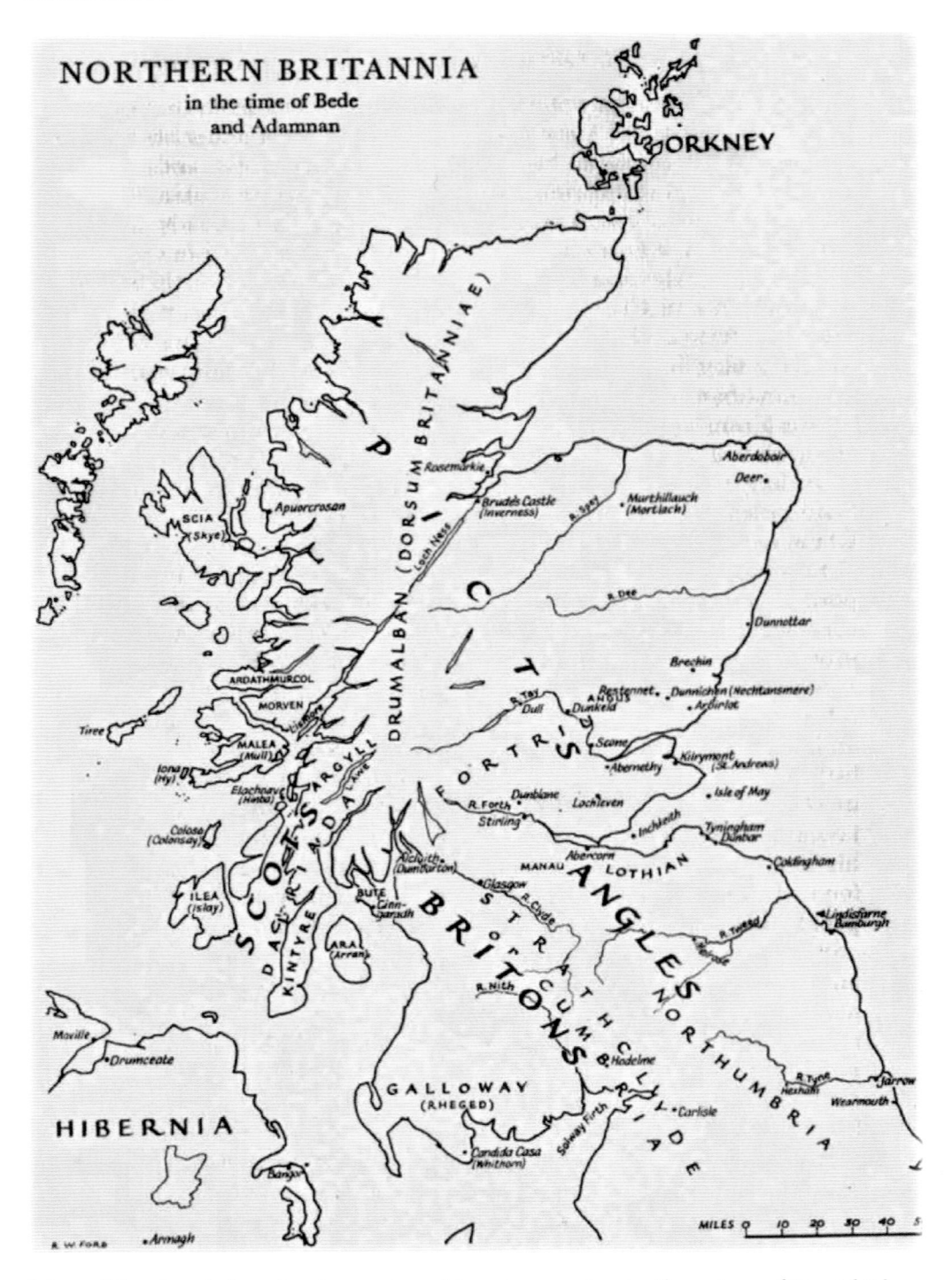

Map of Scotland showing its various kingdoms prior to the reign of David I.[9]

Origins of Names and Places

David I and Ecclesiastical Reform

The recorded history of Mearns Kirk begins in the 12th century in the reign of William I, who was King of Scotland from 1163 to 1214. William was the grandson of King David I (1124-1153) and great grandson of Malcolm III (Canmore) and Queen Margaret, later St. Margaret, who is depicted in one of the large stained glass windows in the church. David and William were cut from the same cloth. David is credited with introducing feudalism to Scotland and William I built upon it. His was the second longest reign of a Scottish monarch prior to the act of Union in 1707, with James VI having the longest reign.

As a young man, David I spent many years at the English Court as his sister Maud had become Queen in 1100. David was knighted by Henry I and created Earl of Huntingdon and through later marriage became the Earl of Northampton, making him a significant English nobleman and landowner. On becoming King of Scotland in 1124 and having been impressed both by the system of government (feudalism) introduced by the Normans in England[8] and by the organisation and growth of the Anglo-Norman Church, he introduced both these secular and religious Norman systems on his return to Scotland.[9] His changes introduced the feudal system of land tenure: he revived old Bishoprics and created new ones and, to secure better government for the Church, divided the country into parishes. His changes in land use and administration amounted to a bloodless Norman conquest of Scotland.

Founding of Paisley Abbey and Mearns Kirk

To help him in the civil and ecclesiastical revival along the lines of the English model, David I brought with him noblemen largely of French descent, who shared in his ideas. He also made use of loyal local princes, chiefs and churchmen - Britons, Scots, Angles and Danes whom he shrewdly did not dispossess in favour of his Anglo-Norman friends, although some of the latter were appointed to high office and others to places where there was no landowner so that improvements could be made.

Of the people that came to Scotland with David I, there is one man that had a special significance for this district and in later centuries, for Scotland. To the Anglo-Norman noble Walter FitzAlan, later to become Hereditary High Steward of Scotland and the founder of the House of Stewart, he gave Renfrewshire, parts of Ayrshire and some land near Kelso. FitzAlan served three Scottish monarchs,

Origins of Names and Places

David I, Malcolm IV and William the Lion before his death in 1177.

In 1163 FitzAlan founded a Cluniac house at Renfrew and a monastery at Paisley, (later to become Paisley Abbey), with monks from an abbey on his lands at Much Wenlock in Shropshire. FitzAlan successfully defended the districts of Renfrew and Paisley against the joint armies of Somerled and the Vikings at the battle of Renfrew in 1164.

Shortly afterwards, an Anglo-Norman church was established at Mearns by a priest, Helia de Perthic, the brother of Robert de Pollok, also known as Robert de Mearns. Helia donated the Anglo-Norman church of Mernes to Paisley Monastery sometime between 1179 and 1199 and is traditionally known as the first minister or priest of Mearns Kirk. Reference to this can be found in the Register of Paisley Abbey and the Register of Glasgow...

[...] *'Donationem illam quam Helias de Perthic eis fecit per consessionem Petri de Polloc fratris Sui de ecclesia de mernes'*

'That donation of Mearns church which Helias made by concession of Peter his brother'[10]

It is believed that this donation was made to allow Helia to enter the Cluniac Order and to benefit from the privileges that order had in the district. It was thought that this priest, Helia de Perthic, later become Canon of Glasgow, and gave his name to the district of modern Glasgow we now know as Partick, but that unfortunately is not true. The district of Glasgow that we know now as Partick was part of the ecclesiastical and administrative centre of David I and had a connection to the parish of Govan just across the river. The name Pertyk appears in official records of the court of David I well before the first appearance of Helia. Helia was the clerk to Herbert, Bishop of Glasgow, 1147-64 and when he was appointed to the Prebend of Perthic in 1162 he takes the name Helia de Perthic and is known as that thereafter.[11] He was therefore already a Canon of Glasgow when he made this donation of the Mearns Kirk to the Monastery at Paisley.

In the old Celtic church at Mearns an altar was dedicated to St. Bride, but when the church was 'Normanised' between 1177-99 AD subsequent altars were added and St. Mary the Virgin joined St. Bride and St. Margaret. These altars were notionally maintained by bequests and donations, for example in 1273 Sir

Herbert de Maxwell endowed St. Mary's altar with:

[…]… *'Six 'Merks' of silver, payable from his Mill in the Auldton of Mearns and provided a chaplain'.*

Captain George Maxwell of Cowglen in 1522 also left the following in his will:

'[…]… Two cows for the support of the altar of St. Bride of Mearns, and one cow for the support of the altar of the Virgin Mary in Mearns…'

The recorded history of Mearns Kirk then starts around 1179 AD. There is no doubt that the interior of the medieval church was very different from today. The most significant difference is that there was no pulpit for the priest to preach from; instead he stood on the altar steps in Roman fashion. Until the beginning of the 18th century there were no pews either for the comfort of the worshippers; if they wished to sit during divine worship, they brought stools with them.

The Knights Templars

About the same time as the new ecclesiastical system was developing, another religious organisation appeared. King David I introduced the Cistercian Order of the Knights Templars to Scotland, a religious military order for the protection of pilgrims to the Holy Land. This order was suppressed in 1307 by order of Pope Clement V on Friday 13 October (if you believe Dan Brown and the Da Vinci Code) and their successors were the Knights Hospitallers, an order of military monks. The Templars had a settlement in Mearns and tradition has it that their chief location was at Capelrig, but they possessed other lands at Newton, Broom, Blackhouse and Southfield (now Mearnskirk Hospital). Capelrig appears on Timothy Pont's map of 1590 but is spelled 'Caplerig', which only adds to the suggestion of a church there. In the graveyard of Mearns Kirk is an ancient gravestone inscribed with a cross and a sword, perhaps that of a Crusader Knight - a Mearns Knights Templar?[12]

Origins of Names and Places

The Maxwells

One of the local chiefs King David I confirmed in office was an Angle named Maccus, whose settlement on the Tweed was Maccus-wiel (pool of Maccus) or Maccus-vil (castle town of Maccus), from which derives the present day name of Maxwell, a name associated with Mearns since the 12th century.

In Mearns another sitting chief confirmed in office was a Gael, Roland de Mearns, whose lordship included the lands of Pollok, both Nether (where Pollok Country Park is now) and Upper (the lands of Pollok Castle Estate which is in the vicinity of the Stewarton and Barrhead roads).

It is thought that Upper and Nether Pollok were not very well managed at the time and for that reason, Walter FitzAlan, Roland's superior, settled three of his vassals there. One of these vassals, Robert, became lord of Mearns at the Auldton, and was succeeded by his son, Nicholas and grandsons Robert and Richard; one of them was the father of Mary de Mearns, the last descendant of that family to bear the name 'Mernes', who married into the Maxwell family. The Maxwells therefore become associated with Mearns and Pollok in or about 1262; Nether and Upper Pollok continued to be under the superiority of Mearns until the 17th century when the titles were sold.

Mearns Castle and Kirk Hill

The present Mearns Castle was built in the 15th century. It is a 'tower house' which is a defensible structure and typical of Scottish gentry houses of the late 14th and 15th centuries. They were normally tall buildings where livestock were kept on the ground floor and the owners slept and lived on wooden floors above. The site may have been used before for the castle of Roland de Mearns in the 12th century, forming the centre of his government. This castle would have been a wooden structure, possibly motte and bailey style. Beside it would be the village where his immediate retainers lived. A castle with its village and church constituted a 'ton' or 'toun' in medieval times. In the 13th century, Mearns Castle and its village were already known as Auldton, a name retained until early last century by a farm beside Mearns Castle. By the 13th century a new 'Ton' had been established further to the west and this was called Newton of Mearns in the 17th and 18th centuries.

Origins of Names and Places

The wooden Newton Castle was built by Sir Herbert de Maxwell before 1273, and was thought to be on Robshill, where the flats known as Robshill Court now stand, but recent excavations there have failed to find any significant archaeology to substantiate this claim. The church of the Newton was probably located at Pollok Castle Estate (Upper Pollok) where, it is recorded, a church or chapel stood until the Reformation. The site was marked by a heap of stones until last century.

The application of the word 'Kirk' to landmarks and buildings occurs throughout ecclesiastical history and there are several examples in this district. Kirkhill for example is thought to relate to a 5th or 6th century church that may have existed in the Auldton. According to Timothy Pont, in his 1590 mapping of this area, there was a 'Kirkton' which was thought to be in the vicinity of Balgray. As explained earlier, the word 'kirk' is a derivation of the Norse word for 'church' and so pre-dates the first written historical references to Mearns Kirk in the 12th Century. It may be that Kirkhill was the site of a church in the 5th or 6th Century, but it is more likely to be the description, abbreviated to Kirkhill, of a small settlement.

It has been quite an interesting exercise to try and push back the timeline for this district and the name of Mearns (or Meirns) as far as possible. Apart from the registers of Paisley Abbey and Glasgow, the only other contemporary document that I have found with any relationship to Mearns is in the *Ragman Rolls* of Edward I. In the rolls there is one signatory whose name I had come across before as residing here; - *Johan Petyt de Miernes* signed the roll and swore allegiance to Edward I in 1296, giving his residence as in the district of the *del counte de Lanark*.

I also began looking for the earliest known maps of the area which show any currently known landmarks or places of interest. I was delighted to find two such maps which can place not only the Church, but the first reference to a village bearing the name 'Neuton', together with a reference to the current Mearns Castle built in 1449; I found also several later maps which refer to Newton of Mearns and Mearns Kirk as place names from which distances are measured.[13]

The earlier maps are those created by Timothy Pont in 1590 and the book published in 1654 by Joan Blaeu based on Pont's drawings. Of the two publications the original hand drawn Pont map for the *'Baronee of Renfrew'* is by far the most interesting, not for its accuracy in relation to proximity of modern places to each other, but for the number of them and the detail with which they are shown.

Origins of Names and Places

The name 'Meirns' appears written on the map in several places which appear to be moorland, and for me confirm the definitions offered earlier for the origins of the name. Mearns Castle is shown as a small structure by comparison to 'Humbie Tower' or to 'Pook' Castle nearby. More curiously it also shows a motte and bailey style castle at Duncarnock Hill, although this may be more a reference to the ruined Iron Age hill fort rather than an occupied structure.

The Pont and Blaeu maps can be accessed via the internet from the National Library of Scotland at the following web addresses:

http://maps.nls.uk/pont/specialist/pont33.html
http://maps.nls.uk/atlas/blaeu/index.html

The relationship between Auldton and Newton Mearns

In the early Middle Ages hamlets appeared at the sites of the castles of the Auldton and the Newton. Sir William Wallace is reputed to have passed through Mearns, via Hazelden, in 1297 and King Edward I of England is said to have been in Mearns Castle and to have issued a writ there on his way from Glasgow to Bothwell in 1301; both occurrences lack foundation in recorded history, but are part of the folklore of this area. By the 16th century the 'Auldton' had declined so much that it is missing altogether from the Pont Map of 1590, to be remembered only as a farm, while the 'Newton' of Mearns grew.

Why was the Newton more successful than the Auldton? There is any number of reasons for this, however I think that the most likely reason is that with the passing of the Mearns family name by marriage into the Maxwell family in the 13th century, the Auldton was no longer considered relevant and was allowed to decline but not to die away altogether.

The village of Mearns was an agricultural community, and remained so for centuries, but by the eighteenth century people were engaged in the textile and dyeing industries. Industry came to the district in the late 17th century. Mills were built to utilise the power of the larger burns and the building of roads brought new opportunities for commerce. 'The Kirkilgat', a landmark in 12th century 'Mernes', followed approximately the same route as today's Mearns Road from Clarkston to the Kirk of Mearns, with a branch going west through the site of the former Shaw Farm and on to Neilston. The part between Mearns Road and Shaw Farm still exists. Over time, this became an increasingly important trade route, first as a bridle path for horses and then as a metalled road for wheeled traffic, passing through the village of 'Mearns' located at Mearns Parish Kirk and on to Kilmarnock and Ayrshire.

This village of Mearns had its own school and its own inn - The Red Lion. Some of the buildings were on what is now the church car park and the school house was on the site now occupied by the present Manse. In 1832 the new Kilmarnock turnpike road was opened. It was built using the latest techniques of the day: Tarmacadam roads. The summits were reduced and the material used to fill the hollows. Tolls were collected at Nellie's Toll - now Eastwood Toll; this is the road we know as the A77 which passes through 'Newton'. This road increased the importance of the 'Newton' for commerce and access to Glasgow, consequently reducing the influence of Mearns Road and like the Auldton before it, it has declined to the point where it carries only local traffic and access nowadays to the main arterial routes of the A77 and M77. The availability of relatively cheap building land adjacent to these two roads, with good connections to Glasgow and beyond, have led to the creation of Newton Mearns as we know it today.

The Reformation

The people of Mearns in the 16th and 17th centuries were closely associated with their Kirk and were Godly people. The great upheavals of the Reformation in Scotland and the teachings of John Knox and John Calvin would leave an indelible mark on their beliefs and faith, producing a literate and questioning society that would be tested repeatedly in the coming decades.

By the sixteenth century the Church in Scotland, as in other countries in Europe, could be described as corrupt. Immorality and neglect of duties were rife. Prelates and priests had strayed far from the path marked out by the early founders of the Church. Many of the great churchmen had more than one benefice and accrued income from each, often not troubling to fulfil their religious duties, preferring instead to lead privileged lives at the royal court. Senior clerics and laymen in the Pre -Reformation Catholic Church abused their positions to secure lucrative livings in the Church for their relatives. The Church had come to be regarded as less of a 'Holy calling' and more like a profession which offered substantial financial gain: for example, James IV conferred the wealthy Bishopric of St. Andrews on his 12 year old son, Alexander; and James V saw to it that a boy of five became Prior of St. Andrews James 1st Earl of Moray; and Mary, Queen of Scots, a mere infant controlled Holyrood and, of course, its revenues. Kelso,

Melrose and Crossraguel Abbeys all poured their wealth into the royal treasury.[14]

In Pre-Reformation times the average parish priest was largely ill-prepared for his post and frequently had little idea of the meaning of the Latin service which he repeated daily. Many faithful churchgoers did not hear a sermon for months at a time. The Council of Trent 1542-63 sought to remedy these flaws, by requiring bishops and rectors to preach at least four times a year; later, this was amended to *'as often as they can do so conveniently'*! A catechism in the Scottish tongue was issued in 1552 to the lesser clergy to help them in the instruction of their congregations in the principal points of the Roman Catholic faith.

Despite all this, it is quite wrong to conclude that every churchman in the first half of the 16th Century was lazy, ignorant and corrupt. Many of the clergy led model lives and tried to live according to their position. Unfortunately, the lives and examples of the majority were eclipsed by the shortcomings of the minority, and despite the best efforts of the Roman Catholic Church in the Lateran and Vatican Councils of the 16th and 17th centuries, to put right some of the worst abuses, the good and bad alike were swept away by the upheaval of 1559-1560 and the start of the Reformation in Scotland.

The Reformation was a slow process in some areas, as in Mearns. It was not until 1572 that a reformed minister, Patrick Adamson, was settled in Paisley with responsibility for Mearns, Neilston and Kilbarchan. In Mearns, the ordinances of the Church, apart from the sacraments, were fulfilled by *'scripture readers'*; exactly how these people were chosen for this duty is unknown, however they performed it from 1574 to 1588 until a permanent minister could be called. In 1588 John Hay was called as Minister of Mearns and he stayed until 1593. He was succeeded by Andrew Hay who *[…]' no ways behaved himself according to his calling…'* and lasted only a year before being succeeded by George Maxwell (1594-1648) the son of the Laird of Auldhouse.

Ministers at this time were required to reside in their parish however George Maxwell chose to reside *'furth of his parish'* and despite the rebuke of the Presbytery continued to do so for many years. The Reformation years were only the start of the religious problems that the parish and the country were to face in the coming century, and the causes of that turmoil are discussed in the next chapter.

Author's Notes

1. For a complete description of this find and the site see *'Excavation of an Early Historic Palisaded Enclosure at Titwood, Mearnskirk, East Renfrewshire'* Authors; Melanie Johnson and Alastair Rees with Ian Ralston.

2. Toolis., Ronan *'Bronze Age pastoral practices in the Clyde Valley: Excavations at West Acres, Newton Mearns'*

3. Toolis., Ronan *'Bronze Age pastoral practices in the Clyde Valley: Excavations at West Acres, Newton Mearns'*

4. Watson, W. J. The History of Celtic Place Names Of Scotland (Edinburgh 1926) Pg., 110-111

5. Gaelic place names of Scotland website, http://www.gaelicplacenames.org/

6. Nicolaisen,W.F.H., Scottish Place Names (New Ed) (J. Donald: Edinburgh 2001) Pg. 140

7. Burleigh, J.H.S., A Church History of Scotland (Oxford University Press; Oxford, 1960), Page 10

8. Debate exists amongst historians of the early Middle Ages as to whether William the Conqueror actually replaced the Anglo-Saxon government with something new. He did bring new laws and legal theories but it seems he adapted the existing administration to his own needs.

9. The map on page 8 shows how Scotland was a divided kingdom in the period 6-9th Centuries AD. Burleigh, J.H.S., A Church History of Scotland (Oxford University Press; Oxford, 1960), Page 20

9. See appendix A for the full Latin text of the Donation and Acceptance, shown in the register of Paisley Abbey.

11. See following link for details. http://poms.cch.kcl.ac.uk/db/record/source/1185/#
    The Bishop bestows on Helia lands that were part of the original bequest by King David I to the Cathedral when it was inaugurated which included islands in the river Clyde opposite the Govan Church estates that were known by the name 'Pertyk'.

12. See Appendix B for a discussion by the author on why this grave marker may not be a Knight Templar's but may in fact be older.

13. John Ainslie., *Map of the County of Renfrew ca.1800* National Library of Scotland

14. Crossraguel Abbey at Maybole in Ayrshire; a daughter house of the Cluniac order founded in 1215, a subordinate house to Paisley Abbey later to have great influence over much of Ayrshire in the 14th and 15th centuries.

Mearns Kirk circa 1900. Notice the small extension of the entrance at clock tower where the Minister would have entered the sanctuary.

From Eaglesham Road with Mr Porter, Postman

The photo above shows the Postman on what is now Eaglesham Road with Mearns Kirk and the Glebe behind him.

Chapter Two:

Challenges to Authority

Middle Ages' monarchs of Europe saw themselves as anointed by God; they had a 'Divine Right' to rule because God had chosen them for that purpose. In 1534, Henry VIII took that premise a stage further and made himself Supreme Head of the Church in England, for political and social reasons.

James VI asserted the supremacy of the Crown over the reformed Scottish Church, and in doing so maintained the 'Divine Right' of kings to rule their subjects as they saw fit, although it has to be said that he did not interfere in the Church's workings or organisation. James' son, Charles I, was brought up in that tradition, which may explain his later attitude towards his English and Scottish subjects. Charles I, however, was no diplomat and in neglecting his Scottish heritage, brought about his own demise. What could cause a growing nation to go from peace and prosperity to revolution and regicide in the space of 25 years? The answer is simple: religion.

The imposition of the Book of Common Prayer on the Scottish Church, introduced against all advice to the contrary, caused uproar. It caused Jenny Geddes to throw her stool at the minister in the pulpit in St. Giles Cathedral in Edinburgh in 1638. This devout Presbyterian was so enraged she was said to have bellowed "De'il gie you colic … fause thief; daur ye say Mass in my lug?" This act of rebellion sparked a riot which led inevitably to armed conflict between the supporters of the National Covenant, who opposed the Crown's attempt to impose Episcopalianism on the Scottish Church, and the King.

Jenny Geddes hurling her stool at James Hannay, Dean of Edinburgh, for daring to read from the Book of Common Prayer.

Challenges to Authority

> *The Evil and Danger of* Prelacy.
>
> A
> # SERMON
> PREACHED AT A
> ## GENERAL MEETING,
> IN THE
> *Black-Fryar-Church* of *Edinburgh*,
> Upon the 13th Day of *June*, 1638,
> AT
>
> THE Beginning of our laft REFORMATION from *Prelacy*, after the Renovation of the NATIONAL COVENANT.
>
> By the Reverend Mr. ANDREW CANT, fometime Minifter of the Gofpel at *Aberdeen*.
>
> 1 PETER v. 3. *Neither as being Lords over God's Heritage: but being enfamples to the Flock.*
>
> GLASGOW,
> Printed for GEORGE PATON, Book-feller in *Linlithgow*. MDCCXLI.

Facsimile of a handbill poster for a sermon about the dangers of Episcopacy; Source: 'The Covenant and Covenanters' Rev. James Kerr (Glasgow 1895)

The National Covenant of 1638 was an idea and a document that was to play a significant role in the coming decades. It set out the principles of Presbyterianism and repudiated any attempt at forcible union with, or replacement by, the Church of England. The oaths taken by the signatories to defend their Kirk were as fundamental to most Scots as the idea itself; they would have none of it, and prepared for war with the Auld Enemy.

The First and Second Bishops' Wars of 1639-1640 followed and were the start of the slippery slope towards regicide.[1] Civil War in England followed shortly thereafter, with Scotland joining the English Parliamentarians in the Solemn League and Covenant of 1643.

Challenges to Authority

The execution of Charles I in 1649 had major ramifications in this district; fines were levied on Royalist sympathisers causing at least one leading family to dispose of property here that they had held for centuries; for example the head of the Maxwell family, the Earl of Nithsdale, was a Royalist. That support cost him so much in fines that he was forced to sell off parts of his estates, including the Barony of Mearns which he sold to Sir George Maxwell of Nether Pollok in 1649. The lairds of Mearns supported the Covenanters, an action which had an important bearing on the future of the congregation of Mearns Kirk.

The wars of the National Covenant, 1643-49 and the uprising in Scotland against Cromwell's rule in 1650-51 brought further bloodshed and misery to the people of Scotland. Desperate for a figurehead that they could mould to their will, the Scots settled with Charles II, proclaiming him King in 1649 at Edinburgh, but before they would allow him to ascend to the throne he had to accept the Solemn League and Covenant and promise to establish Presbyterianism throughout Britain. And if that was not enough, prior to his coronation in 1651 and while he was still at sea on his way back from exile in France to Scotland, he was subjected to an ordeal by Presbyterian commissioners on the mistakes of his father, on matters of faith and on the duties of a Covenanted King. This became known as the 'Grand Remonstrance' as this contemporary satirical cartoon shows.

In years to come the memory of this indignation would haunt Charles II and explains partly his later behaviour towards the Scottish Kirk, particularly here in the West and South West of Scotland, the source of much of the ideas for the Grand Remonstrance.

Contemporary cartoon of the manner of the Grand Remonstrance being given to Charles II in 1651 before his Coronation. Source: Glasgow University, Special collections, via Internet

Challenges to Authority

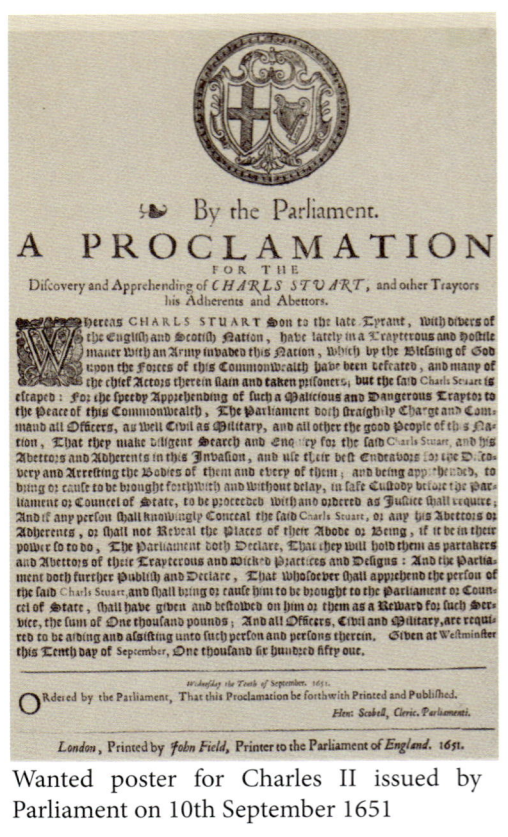

At his coronation at Scone in January 1651, the Scots proclaimed Charles to be King of Scotland, France, England and Ireland. His reign, this time, was short lived. In trying to reclaim his throne by force of arms, the Scots army that invaded England in 1651 was defeated by Cromwell's forces at the Battle of Worcester. Charles II managed to flee to France yet again and as many a Scots monarch before him, bide his time well.

He did not have long to wait. The Interregnum, as it has become known, was an austere and joyless time for everyone. Scotland meanwhile was ruled by Major General George Monck, who had fought with Cromwell and defeated the Covenanters at the Battle of Dunbar in 1652. For the first time in history, an English army was able to assert effective control over Scotland. Monck and James Sharp, a minister from Crail, later had a hand in organising the restoration of Charles II in 1660. Cromwell was a superb tactician and military leader but no politician - and neither was his son Richard. On Cromwell's death in 1658 the country was in political and social turmoil; his son Richard as his successor struggled to exert any authority as Lord Protector of the Commonwealth and the scene was set for the return of the King once more.

Wanted poster for Charles II issued by Parliament on 10th September 1651

Disposition of armies at the battle of Worcester, 3 September 1651

Challenges to Authority

Charles II returned to the throne with a long memory and an unforgiving nature. One of his first acts was to pass the 'Recession Act', of 1660, which repealed all the legislation passed by the Commonwealth Government. He commissioned a new version of the Book of Common Prayer, published in 1662; this version is the subject of a major exhibition this year (2012) at Hampton Court Palace in London.

During this time, Mearns Kirk was served by two refugee ministers from Ireland displaced by Monck's campaigns: Hugh Cunningham and David Gemmill. Nothing is known about their time here. In 1652 John Burnett, chaplain to Lord Wemys, was called to Mearns, but we cannot establish if he actually came here. In 1653 a well-liked Minister settled in Mearns - the Rev. William Thomson, who was later to be victimised by agents of Charles II.

The following 28 years (1660-1688) was a period of violence and persecution of the Presbyterian Church by Charles II. The Middleton Act of 1662 abolished Presbyterianism, established Episcopacy as the state religion and included the imposition of bishops on the Scottish clergy. It also abolished lay patronage (appointment of ministers by the patron of the parish) and sought to impose conformity and obedience in the Church by the use of the newly commissioned Book of Common Prayer, forcing ministers who would not accept this new order, out of their livings:

[…] *'all who had entered there on their charges since 1649, when patronage was abolished, must quit their churches and manses unless they were presented by the lawful patron and inducted in episcopal order before 1st November 1662…'* [2]

Failure to do so resulted in military intervention, consequently all Kirk Sessions, Presbyteries and Synods were abolished; individual rights of assembly and worship were under attack.

The Origins of the Non Conformists

The following decades were full of tragic periods, each marked with a new persecution of covenanted ministers and their congregations, and an escalation in personal violence. The main source of grievance was the legislation passed to control religious practices. The passing of the *'Act of Fines'* in 1662 was one such act, which affected everyone. The purpose of this act was to enforce attendance at church; the result was somewhat different and not entirely unexpected. The congregations of dispossessed ministers responded by non-attendance and open air worship.

In 1663, William Thomson, the Minister of Mearns mentioned earlier, was turned out of his ministry and manse for non-conformity; this occurred in winter with ensuing hardship to him and his family. Thereafter, the parish was held by a succession of four 'Curates or Prelates' or conforming Episcopalian ministers, who were put there by the State and retained there by force of arms, banishments, fines and other means designed to punish the people of the parish for non-attendance at church. The Curates were detested by the people, who stayed away, preferring instead to attend the meetings of the dispossessed ministers who contrived, against the law, to preach and perform the services of marriage and baptism.

The people suffered most of all. Some were brought before the civil courts and fined although the nobles suffered too. In the neighbouring parish, Sir George Maxwell of Nether Pollok was fined and, in 1665, imprisoned for 4 years for non-attendance. Following the battle at Rullion Green near Edinburgh in 1666, between a force of Covenanters, of whom several were from Mearns, and Royal troops under General Tam Dalyell, ten of those who surrendered on a promise that their lives would be spared were betrayed and hanged, among them being John Shields of Titwood and John Parker of Busby.

In 1669 the Crown passed an Act preventing conventicles…

[…]that these meetings are the rendezvouses of rebellion, and tend in a high measure to the disturbance of the public peace, doth therefore, with advice and consent foresaid, statute and declare, that whosoever, without licence or authority foresaid, shall preach, expound scripture, or pray, at any of those meetings in the field, or in any house where there be more persons than the house contains, so as some of them be without doors (which is hereby declared to be a field conventicle) or who shall convocate any number of people to these meetings, shall be punished with death, and confiscation of their goods.[3]

The provisions of this act would be ruthlessly imposed in the coming decades, but that still did not force people back to the church and, in 1670, Robert Fleming, the 'Curate' in Mearns declared that '…*The people did much withdraw from hearing and baptizing*' that he had '…*No session and the fabric of the Kirk was in a ruinous condition…*' In the same year Mr George Birnie of Kilallen

Challenges to Authority

Parish also registered similar complaints. He gave as the reason that

'…The Laird of Barrochan did entertain Mr James Wallace, Minister of Mearns, who constantly preached in Barrochan and before his coming the people had been orderly.…'

From this we can see that the non-conforming ministers at Mearns were in the forefront of religious thought and discussion and perhaps more importantly the people followed them willingly.

James Wallace was probably the non-conforming minister at Mearns ministering to the people who refused the services of Mr Fleming. In 1673 Sir George Maxwell of Newark (Nether Pollok?) was fined £94,800 Scots for absence from church, and as a heritor he was especially vulnerable… […] *'And, as to all heritor's and others aforesaid, who shall be present at any of these field-conventicles, it is hereby declared, they are to be fined, toties quoties, in the double of the respective fines appointed for house conventicles; but prejudice of any other punishment due to them by law as seditious persons and disturbers of the peace and quiet of the kirk and kingdom…'*[4]

Based on the above rules the fines were levied as follows;

[..] 'For each Sabbath's absence from the parish church for three years……………	£31,200
For each Sabbath's attendance at conventicle ………………………………………	£62,400
For three 'disorderly' baptisms, that is children baptised by an 'Outed' Minster....	£ 1,200
Total.....	£94,800 [5]

The bill was made up in the following manner; a fine for absence from church on Sunday; a double fine for attendance at a conventicle; and a further fine for unauthorised baptisms. Sir John Maxwell of Nether Pollok was fined £93,000 Scots in the same year.[6]

So then, apart from the doctrinal issues, why were the 'Curates' so unpopular? Barr gives several reasons, but his quotation from Bishop Burnet, via McCrie, is perhaps the best description available, […] *'They were the worst preachers I ever heard; they were ignorant to a reproach, and many of them were openly vicious. They were a disgrace to their orders and the sacred function, and were, indeed, dregs and refuse of the northern parts'*[7]

Challenges to Authority

The people were instead gathering in the open on the moors at 'Conventicles'. In 1672 these conventicles were held at Mearns Castle, but three years later in 1675 a garrison occupied the castle and the worshippers took to the moors an increasingly dangerous undertaking, as the following extract shows;

[…] *'And it is hereby offered and assured, that if any of his majesty's good subjects shall seize and secure the persons of any who shall either preach or pray at these field-meetings, or convocate any persons thereto, they shall, for every such person so seized and secured, have five hundred merks paid unto them for their reward, out of his majesty's treasury, by the commissioners thereof, who are hereby authorised to pay the same; and the said seizers and their assistants are hereby indemnified for any slaughter that shall be committed in the apprehending and securing of them…* [8]

It was open season on Presbyterians. Trust became paramount: given the rewards for informing on your neighbour, no wonder that the *'Corresponding Societies'* such as at Mearns and Fenwick took their security seriously. The moors were common land and the holding of conventicles there implicated no one other than themselves. Some were caught and imprisoned, others were heavily fined and Mearns received a detachment of the 'Highland Host', an army of 9,000 or so made up of Highlanders and lowland militias, but mainly from the Episcopalian north of Scotland who had orders to find themselves billets wherever they pleased and not at their own expense. As many as 20 were quartered in one house of the Laird at Hawthornden as a punishment, he thereafter had to feed them for as long as they were there; other houses were similarly victimised. The government said that their purpose was to *'keep the peace'* but most people saw in it a deliberate attempt to provoke rebellion and so provide a good excuse for the harshest treatment of the populace and especially Covenanters.

On May 3rd 1679 the senior Scottish Episcopalian cleric, Archbishop James Sharp, former minister at Crail, was murdered on Magus Moor near St Andrews. This murder marked the start of the War of the Covenants during which the battles of Drumclog (1st June 1679) and Bothwell Brig (22nd June 1679) were fought; Drumclog was a surprising victory for the Covenanters and Bothwell Brig a sad defeat. Several Mearns men took part in these and other battles, with the fugitives from Bothwell Brig being listed and searched for. These included William Wilson and John Gilmore of Mearns; Jon Fouls of Newton; James Grey of Mearns Castle; and Robert Pollok, servant at Flinder. A Hamilton of Greenbank survived the battle and escaped.

Challenges to Authority

In 1681 the Test Act[9] was passed, which prescribed an oath to be taken by all holding public office in Church and State. Implicit in this oath was a repudiation of the obligations of the National Covenant and the acceptance of Charles II as Head of the Church, despite the fact that Charles had been excommunicated the previous year by Rev. Donald Cargill at Torwood in Stirlingshire. The Act was held in ridicule by Covenanters and so the persecution went on unabated, this time under the leadership of the Duke of York, a staunch Roman Catholic.

During this time Captain John Paton, one of the leaders of the Covenanters, who had commanded a troop of horse at Rullion Green and had been on the run for 20 years, was captured in the district. He was taken at Floak Farm in the Parish of Mearns in 1684 and executed in Edinburgh in the following year. Mearns men were fined, imprisoned or banished to plantations in the Americas for non-attendance at church, including James Pollok, Laird of Balgray; James Hamilton of Langton; John Rankin of Tofts, and John Fauls of Newton. These place names are well known to us, some in their original context as names of farms and others now as names of streets or housing areas.

The religious persecution of anyone suspected of being a Covenanter was so pervasive that it even reached into a man's house [...] ...*'James Algie and John Park were tenant farmers at a small holding at Kennishead, they were taken in their house by soldiers as they were about to engage in family worship, on being told to take the Abjuration Oath and the Test which affirmed the king's supremacy in all causes, ecclesiastical as well as civil...'* [10]

They declined, saying [...]... *'As one oath would not save them from the other, they would take no oath at all...'* and were executed at Paisley Cross a few hours later. This complete disregard of the rights of the individual was only brought to an end by the Revolution of 1688 with the accession of William of Orange and Queen Mary and the Revolution Settlement of 1690.

In 1685, the third of the 'Curates' in Mearns was John Taylor. The people for the most part ignored him and withheld their financial support from him, including George Pollok of Waterfoot and James Wylie of Flinder, whom he summonsed for arrears of stipend.[11]

In 1687, Elias Paul, *'Sheriff-officer in ye Mearns and Precentor at ye Kirk of Mearns'*... cited a substantial number of the parishioners for non-payment of marriage and baptism dues. The last 'Curate' in Mearns was James Inglis (1686-

1688). The Covenanters left him alone and met elsewhere, calling their own minister. Following the Revolution of 1688, the Covenanters looked forward to religious freedom. The Test Act of 1681 was repealed in July 1690 and those ministers that had been evicted in favour of 'conformists' were reinstated.[12] In recognition of and restitution for the sufferings of the Mearns people, the laird of Upper Pollok was knighted and in 1703, created a baronet - Sir Robert Pollok of Pollok.

The Secession

With the Revolution Settlement of 1690, the Church of Scotland re-emerged unaffected by so many fiery trials: the emblem of this triumph, the Burning Bush and the motto *'nee tamen consumebatur'* - 'Yet it was not consumed' now appeared on the Acts of the General Assembly, an allusion to Exodus 3:2. From this date on the people of the parish led much more peaceful lives and were at liberty to worship without hindrance from king or state.

The memories and fervour of the days of persecution remained with many in the parish, memories of a spirituality which they feared was now fading from the Church. They sensed decay in the restoration of parish and church courts, and those who experienced this disappointment decided to do something about it. It has been mentioned how, in 1687, the last 'curate' was ignored by the majority of the people of Mearns and how they called their own Minister, John Glen. This was only one instance of the actions of many such unofficial groups of people, especially in south-west Scotland. Although in constant danger and often broken up and their members punished and even killed, those 'Societies', as they were known, acted as 'shadow' sessions and even 'shadow' courts of the Church. Admission was scrupulously limited to those who adhered to the Covenants; aspiring members were subjected to searching questions to shut out spies or persons morally and doctrinally unworthy. Some of them were the followers of Richard Cameron - the first 'Cameronians.' They deplored a church that no longer carried the banner of the Covenants. They with others of similar outlook formed their own Presbytery in 1745 and became the Reformed Presbyterian Church and by doing so brought about the first Secession.[13]

Since the days of the Solemn League and Covenant (1643), there had been a 'Society' in Mearns and together with similar societies in Fenwick, Eaglesham, Neilston and other localities, it was a unit in the 'correspondence' (a group of Societies) of Fenwick. In 1739 the Mearns Society acceded to the Secession

Church and so founded the Newton church, which today we know as Newton Mearns Parish Church. Since then the Newton congregation has had four churches and four manses; over the same period Mearns Kirk has had two church buildings and three manses[14.]

Peace at Last and Freedom of Worship

During the Jacobite Rebellions the parish remained loyal to the king and there was little support for the Pretenders. In 1724 [...] *'within the Red Lion at Mearnskirk a Cumbernauld carrier proposed a toast to King James VIII, whereupon Robert Clark who dwelt at Kirkhill and was an elder forbye, did assault him, striking and wounding him to the effusion of blood, and all out of loyalty to King George.'*

The Kirk Session records are silent on any of the Jacobite intrigues, there is however a gap in the records during the 1715 uprising and again during the 1745 uprising. The surviving Minute Book, currently at the National Archives, shows that the Session Minutes stopped in January 1715 and started again in the same book in 1716, similarly again in 1745-46 the records are silent. Given the information to hand the above silences on the Kirk Session records are not surprising. It seems that the Kirk Session has in the past had a habit of irregular meetings, and on at least one occasion died out altogether which resulted in a petition to the presbytery in Paisley in 1855 for the imposition of a Kirk Session and elders at Mearns Kirk by them because…

[...] *that for several years past there has been no elders in said parish in connection with the Church of Scotland and consequently no Kirk session'*…

The reason given in the complaint for this action was so that the retiring collection monies could be accounted for, no Kirk Session equates to no offerings.[15]

The session records give a snapshot of the congregation and the moral position of the congregation and by inference, society in the district. The main focus of the Kirk Session here, from the surviving records, shows that they were wholly devoted to inquiries into the sex lives of their congregation; gossip was on occasion the excuse for individuals being brought before the Kirk Session to have their intimate relations discussed. Not only was the nature of their 'adulterous' relations discussed, but they were punished by being 'excoriated'[16] by the congregation in the church over a specified period. The same problem existed then as today: the provision for maintenance of any children conceived before they became a financial burden on the parish; however some people would not just take a telling and appear with regularity in the records of the session. Sometimes the ecclesiastical courts could impose a monetary fine on the miscreant, known as 'Buttock Mail' for having sex out of wedlock. So far there are no records to suggest that this practice was adopted here.

What is surprising is that in the times before organised Poor Laws were created in England, Scotland had its own version of a Poor Law that dated from 1595. There are entries in the parish records from the early 1700's that relate to payments made by the church to local farmers to transport un- or under- employed farm workers to Fenwick and Stewarton from the parish, together with detailed records of others in the parish who perhaps through illness or death of the breadwinner were unable to work, receiving charity relief from the church on a weekly basis. The notes and records for these transactions cover a period of about 4 years and are quite detailed, showing incomes from wealthy parishioners and outgoings in the form of relief.

By the end of the eighteenth century Mearns Kirk had suffered – and survived - the ravages of the Killing Time and the divisions of Secessionists that had split it into two distinct congregations, which differed substantially in belief and practice and would not be reunited again under a single administration for nearly two hundred years.

Author's Notes

1. For a complete account of the Civil Wars in the three Kingdoms see 'The Civil Wars; A Military history of England Scotland and Ireland 1638-1660' Kenyon and Ohlmeyer (Oxford University press 1998)
2. Barr, James. The Scottish Covenanters Pg. 45(John Smith and Son, Glasgow 1946)
3. www.Project Gutenberg.org   Act against Conventicles, section 18 http://www.gutenberg.org/the_national_convenants3
4. Project Gutenberg.org, Act against Conventicles 1669
5. Barr, James. The Scottish Covenanters (John Smith and Sons :Glasgow 1946) Pg.98
   Currency conversion rates from old Scots money into English pounds

1 pistole	=	12 pounds
1 half pistole	=	6 pounds
1 dollar	=	4 merks
	=	56 shillings
1 pound / £	=	20 shillings
1 merk	=	14 shillings
1 half merk	=	7 shillings
1 quarter merk	=	3 shillings, 6 pence
1 shilling / s.	=	12 pence
1 bawbee	=	6 pence
1 turner or bodle	=	2 pence
1 pence /d.		

   The original value of the merk minted in the reign of Charles II was 13s 4d; in 1681 it was raised to 14s (the 4 merk piece rose accordingly from 53s 4d to 56s). Gold pistoles were only minted in 1701. Shillings circulated in coins of 5s, 10s, 20s, 40s, and 60s. After the Act of Union, 1707, Scotland's real money and its money of account were by law uniform with those of England. <[http://www.pierre-marteau.com/currency/converter/eng-sco.html]>
6. Ibid Pg. 46
7. McCrie, II pages 92,93
8. Project Gutenberg.org, Act against Conventicles 1669
9. For the requirement of the Test Act, see the following link [http://www.rps.ac.uk/trans/1681/7/29]
10. Barr, James. The Scottish Covenanters (John Smith and Sons :Glasgow 1946) Pg.98

    The abjuration oath was a requirement to say 'God save the King' usually at gun point, failure to do so marked the subject out as a Covenanter (who could not say it because of his or her beliefs). The resulting punishment was death, the executioner being absolved in law of all responsibility for it and rewarded.
11. Not as unusual an occurrence as one might think, and not restricted to the 17th Century either, there are several instances of this action being taken by sitting Ministers against the Heritors of the Church in the 19th Century. Their writs are in the National Archive of Scotland.
12. www.rps.ac.uk/trans/1690/4/43
13. For a detailed explanation of the secessions and how each group related to each other doctrinally see J.H.S Burleigh, A Church History of Scotland (Oxford University Press, Oxford: 1960)
14. For a discussion of the secession see A Boyd-Scott., Old Days and Ways in Newton Mearns Chap 3 and 4.
15. Gilmour, Allan. 'Memorandum to Paisley Presbytery' 29 November 1855, MPK, Kirk Session Papers
16. 'Excoriation' or public rebuke and humiliation could be avoided by the payment of 'Buttock Mail' a means by which a monetary fine could be imposed on someone found guilty in an Ecclesiastical Court – Wikipedia

The Mearns Kirk Building - Past and Present

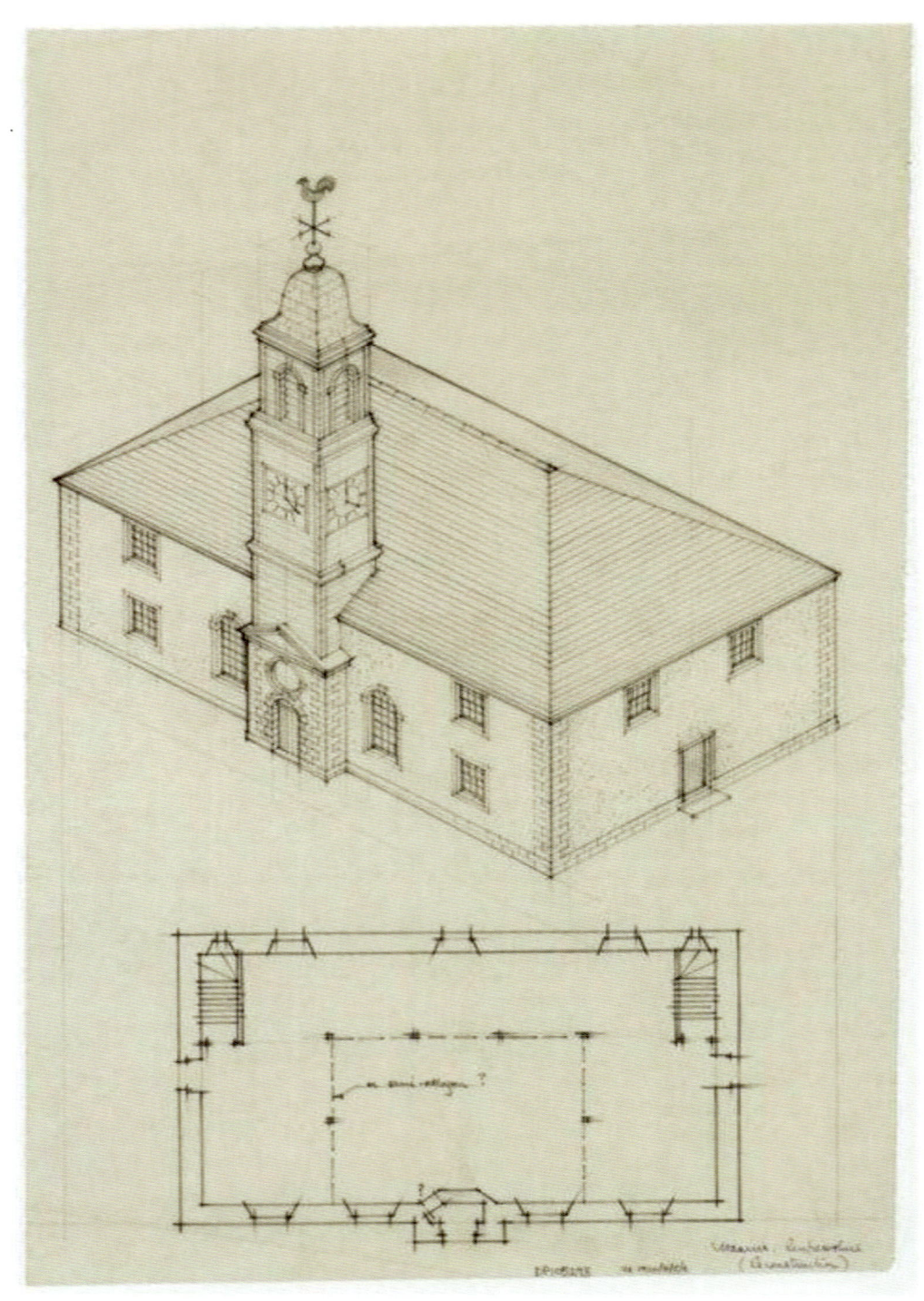

Preparatory drawing of Church building prior to renovation in 1932[1]

Chapter Three:

The Mearns Kirk Building Past and Present

The main point of this chapter is to describe as far as I can the history of the church building. This building has undergone repair and renovation over the years since it was constructed in 1813 and I have found evidence that suggests the shape of the previous building that stood here prior to 1813. The most obvious questions to be answered here is why is the current church a square building? What went before it? And is it all new?

The shape of church buildings in pre Reformation times was important and was normally cruciform, as representing the shape of the cross. That shape was important in Christian tradition in that it symbolically represented the union of the people with Christ's suffering on the cross. Traditional Christian church buildings were normally positioned with an east / west aspect. Those that had been built in predominantly Pagan or pre Christian times and later absorbed into the Christian tradition were generally north / south in aspect, as Mearns Kirk is now. Prior to the renovations the minister led the worship from a pulpit on what is now the back or south wall.

After the Reformation in Scotland, the shape of any new church building was unimportant: the important part of the ceremony was in hearing the word of God, and not the relationship between the building and any altars that may have been there. Therefore any new building in post reformation Scotland could be any shape it liked, but mostly they are square because that shape is the easiest and cheapest to build.

In starting my search I was reliant on several, at times contradictory, secondary sources. These sources suggested that the current building is larger than that which preceded it by a considerable margin and was enlarged to allow for the increase in size of congregation, and it is on that basis thought to be a completely new structure. Although I would not take that contention too literally, as there is ample evidence in the fabric of the building itself to suggest that at least part of the original structure has been retained. For those of you who are not familiar with the orientation of the church, the north wall of the church is where the chancel now sits, the south wall is where the tower is and the two large stained glass windows are, the east door, which is the main entrance to the church, gives access through what was previously the vestry.

The current layout of the church dates from the 1932 renovation. Prior to this the minister would enter via a door in the clock tower, which is now the back wall. The drawing on the page 1 of this chapter shows the exterior of the church building prior to the alterations of the 1930s. The main changes proposed in the alterations to the church in 1932, the most significant changes to the building since its construction in 1813, were the creation of the chancel, vestry and session house and the re-ordering of the gallery floor above into two wings. The gallery floor was a departure from the existing design, which according to a 1913 photograph shows that the upper gallery may have been a 'U' shape.

Again, some of what follows here is taken from the 1982 booklet, together with my own research and that of Mr James Gilchrist into the architecture of the building and the changes made during the renovations. The drawings of the church building that accompany this chapter have been obtained from the Canmore Archive of the 'Royal Commission on the Ancient and Historical Monuments of Scotland', helpfully shortened to RCAHMS and can be found at this website: http://www.canmore.rcahms.gov.uk

It has proved to be a useful resource in investigating the history of the architecture of the building since 1813. The church building is listed on the RCAHMS website and it has a rather unflattering description - which may be the origins of all the confusion regarding the building…

[…] *a two storey box with clock tower, resulting from the complete remodelling of a late 16th century church; recent chancel and wings.*

In our own time the subject of the church's history and positioning has attracted the attention of others, such as the Rev. A. Boyd-Scott who in his book on the history of the village of Newton Mearns states that […] *the configuration of the site is not without signs of having been defined and shaped in Celtic times…* this alludes to the north/ south alignment discussed earlier.

The Mearns Kirk Building - Past and Present

Mearns Kirk viewed from the air showing graveyard and extensions

The aerial picture shows the use of the land within the graveyard. At the west end of the church building, an area has not been used for any internments, the land here is much higher than the wall that can be seen surrounding the church yard; the presumption here is that this vacant area is an outcrop of rock that was therefore unsuitable for use as part of the graveyard.

The graveyard itself has recently been the subject of a history project to record all the information on the gravestones and other markers before they are lost to the effects of the weather and time. The earliest gravestone that is legible dates from 1611. The results of the project are available online and can be found at the following website: http://www.mearnskirkyardproject.co.uk/ An index to individual graves is displayed on a board beside the path at the south side of the church building.

The current church building has been the subject of some speculation over the years as to whether it has been completely rebuilt or has been remodelled and extended. The problem with existing sources on this point seems to come from conflicting entries in the statistical accounts of the parish written in the 18th and 19th centuries as well as the RCAHMS catalogue entry.

The Mearns Kirk Building - Past and Present

The first entry regarding the church building relates to that made by the minister of Mearns, the curate Robert Fleming mentioned in Chapter Two, who complains about the state of the building, but does not record whether the building was renovated thereafter. Neither do the parish records. The second more confusing entry comes from Rev. George McLatchie in the 1791 '**Old Statistical Account of Scotland**' […] '*A very good Manse was built in 1789 and the church was fitted up in a very neat and commodious manner in 1792...*' so we know that at least some work was carried out before the 1813 renovations. The second entry comes from the '**New Statistical Account of Scotland**' dated 1834 and is by the Minister Rev. Donald MacKellar ' […] *the parish church contains about 600 sittings, is in a good state of repair and is centrically enough sited, the glebe contains 4 acres, and a new Manse is being built at a cost of £1,300 Scots money...*'

These comments are hardly surprising given that the building would only have been 15 years old at the most.

To further confuse matters and as part of a regular updating of the records of the parish, there was a further account of the building given in Francis H Groome's '**Statistical Account of Scotland 1881**' […] '*the parish church ¾ mile south east of Newton Mearns is a very old building, altered and enlarged in 1813 with 730 sittings, Clock tower and spire...*'

So there you have it, depending on what source you read, the building is either old, very old or new. I think that it is a mixture of both and still retains part of the previous structure.

There are also those items that are in the fabric of the church building, such as the stone in the east wall dated 1667. It is thought to relate to a marriage between two local families; is it a part of the original fabric of the building? I would suggest that it is not part of the original building fabric for the following reason. Marriage stones were normally placed in the houses of newly married couples, and there is a well-established European tradition for this. However, I have learned from an older parishioner that the stone came from the rubble of a demolished house used to create the walls.

Given the contradictory nature of the sources, it is little wonder that confusion exists as to why a new, larger building was required in 1813 if, given that a mere 20 or so years earlier, Rev. McLatchie was describing the existing one as in 'good repair'. The reason for the new building is due, I think, to the influx of people to

Marriage Stone from the Restoration Period, East Wall

the new industries being started here, such as the Bleachfields and the Dye works near to Blackhouse Farm, together with the construction of the new toll road that ran through the Newton.

Furthermore, was the building completely demolished and the current building erected in its place? Could it be that the description by Mr Groome has it correct in saying that the building was altered and enlarged? I cannot find the sources for his information in any of the national archives, so must presume that this information is no longer available, although this was an interesting premise that was worthy of additional research.

There is a discrepancy in the size of the building too, as the sittings increase over the period 1813-1881, with no reference to any structural alterations to the fabric of the building until the 20th century. How then did 600 sittings in 1834 become 730 sittings by 1881 if there had not been a substantial alteration at some point in the intervening years? It could be explained by the reduction in size of the division of the church per square foot, as allocated by seat rents, with a consequent reduction in space, or it could be that the upstairs part of the church was either added to the building or enlarged to accommodate more people. I know of one family that gave up part of their pew to accommodate the communion table when it was installed in 1913, but so far have been unable to find any other information from Kirk Session records on a reduction of seating space.

The Mearns Kirk Building - Past and Present

The Previous Building

Interested in the contention that the building had been altered and enlarged, I set about looking for evidence of the shape of the previous building. In trying to find out that shape I looked at the various churches in the area that have survived from that time. I took a 7 mile radius from Mearns Kirk as a sample and had a look at some of these buildings on the surviving maps from the late 18th Century and early 19th centuries for any similarities to Mearns Kirk.

What struck me most when looking at the Neilston church, was the similarities between the two buildings: regarding overall shape, window style and the placement of the main door through the tower. My curiosity was further aroused after a lecture at Giffnock Library by an archaeologist from the National Trust for Scotland who pointed me in the right direction. The source of this information can be found on '*William Roy's Military Map of Scotland*' currently available online from the National Library of Scotland, and which shows the shape of the old kirk.

The shape of the old Mearns Kirk was 'T' shaped, with the north wall being the main body and the short arm of the letter 'T' being the steeple tower. The shape of it is given on the colour version of the '*William Roy Military Map 1747-55 The Lowlands of Scotland, District of Renfrew in the Parish of Mearns*'. Here the shape of the old church building and outhouses as well as the Manse is shown in colour together with their boundaries.

The term 'complete re-modelling' used by previous publications to describe the renovations of 1813 is, I think, misleading. The church at Neilston is the same general shape and I would suggest that the remodelling of Mearns Kirk in 1813 followed its example and in best Presbyterian traditions the builders reused what they could first and added on later.

So my suggestions about the original building are that a small part of the east wall including the door, a similar amount of the west wall and door, together with the main tower door, date from before the 1813 renovations. The previous building was a long low roofed structure that had been transformed into the present building by squaring off the shape. This was done by rebuilding both the north and south walls in their current positions and by raising the height of the east and west walls and adding a new roof. These changes would account for the description of the church in the 1881 Statistical Account mentioned earlier that

The Mearns Kirk Building - Past and Present

described the church as being 'very old', quite! It also accounts for the removal of some grave stones at the south wall that show obvious signs of having been disturbed at some time in the past to where they are now. It struck me as odd why a minister would be walking on grave stones. Where was the footpath? Why not use the main door in the east wall? As there was now no space on the graveyard site to walk on, the only explanation that I could come up with was that the previous path lies inside the church building, and as a consequence those graves that were outside the line of the building would have to be moved to accommodate the new structure. I had hoped to find evidence of this in the Kirk Session minutes but there are no records for that time.

The diagram below is what I think happened during the alterations of 1813. The walls marked in black were removed to floor level, those marked in green were retained, including the door facades, and those marked in red built to their present height.

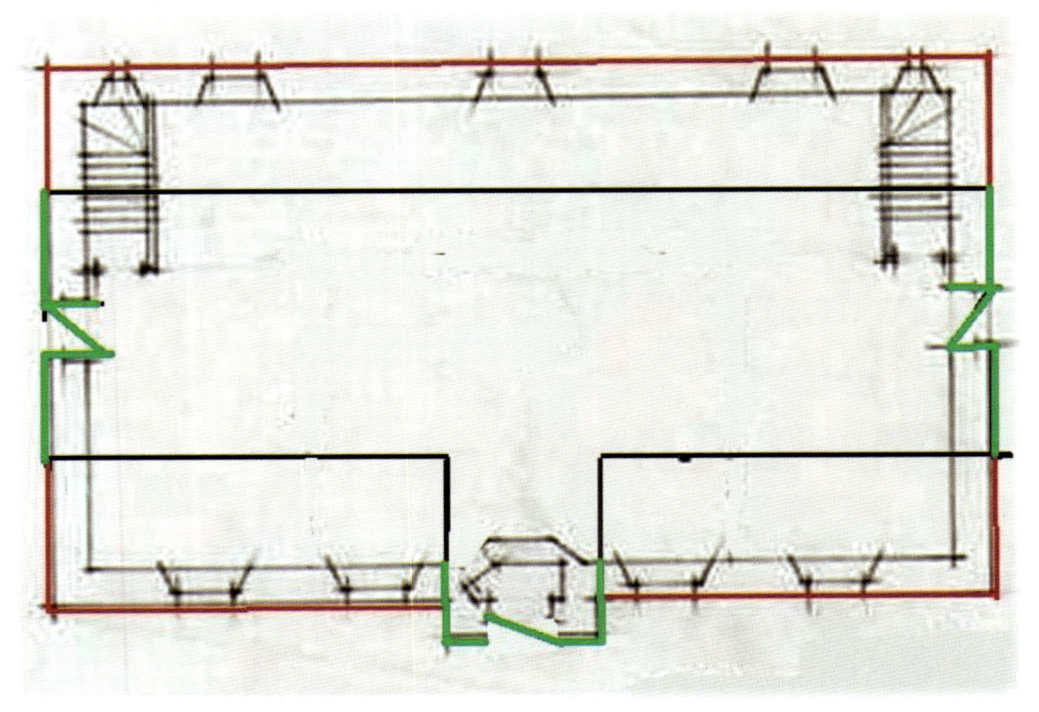

The Mearns Kirk Building - Past and Present

The facades shown in the photographs opposite show a style of architecture that was popular in the 18th century, known as 'Renaissance style' and would fit with the evidence given by the Rev. McLatchie (1788-1833) that there had been work done to the building in the late eighteenth century.

The date carved on the keystone at the vestry door refers to the re-dedication of the building after the 1813 renovations; the style of the doors and exterior of the building especially at the clock tower are reminiscent of Pollok House, at Pollok Park.

The connection and the influence of the Pollok family with the church in the 18th and 19th centuries in terms of patronage are well known, and the adoption of this style may show their influence.

The Mearns Kirk Building - Past and Present

Mearnskirk circa 1890, viewed from the road

The above photograph is perhaps the best example of the church building before any major works had been carried out. Note in the foreground at the tower that there is a porch; if you look at the photograph of the tower door on the previous page you can still see the roofline markings on the wall above the door. The building seen here exhibits the Renaissance style of architecture so popular in the late eighteenth and early nineteenth centuries with symmetry of style around the central clock tower and its classical façade. This building is in keeping with the style of country houses in this district. Compare the building above with Greenbank House and Pollok House, both within 5 miles, and the similarities become obvious.

Pollok House

Greenbank House

The Renovations of 1932

The renovations were instigated by the Rev. David Scott in 1927. The occasion for raising the issue with the church building stems from repairs to the manse which was raised at a Kirk Session meeting in the church hall in Ayr Rd on 4th November 1927, when the state of the fabric of the church building was discussed, along with the remedy.

It appears from the minutes, that the floor of the church was in dire need of replacement due to rising damp and the lack of a damp proof course. Given that the building was erected in 1813 and damp proof courses were not common building practice at that time this is not surprising, what is though was that it took so long to fail, consequently, as the session minutes note…

[…] the complete floor requires to be removed and this would entail excavating the ground under the present floor as there was no air space under the present floor and the excavated surface would require to be asphalted before a new floor could be laid.'[2]

This was a major upheaval for the congregation, which was experiencing a period of growth in members as the session minutes note. However, the minister David Scott, seeing the opportunity that presented itself to have the alterations and repairs to the building carried out at the same time urges the Kirk Session to […] *take into serious consideration the question of the complete renovation of the inside of the church and the addition of a vestry as there was no vestry and suitable office…*' What is not immediately apparent from the minutes is that it would take a further four years and a change of minister before the renovations were commenced.

The church closed on 15 March 1931 and the congregation met in the church halls for the duration of the renovations. Newton Mearns Parish Church assisted with Communion during July and August of 1931 by allowing use of their church. Mearns Kirk reopened on 13 March 1932. The renovations followed the plans shown here and completely changed the orientation of the congregation from south to north facing, removed part of the upper gallery creating two wings as we have today as well as changing the colour of the wooden fittings from dark to light oak.

The Mearns Kirk Building - Past and Present

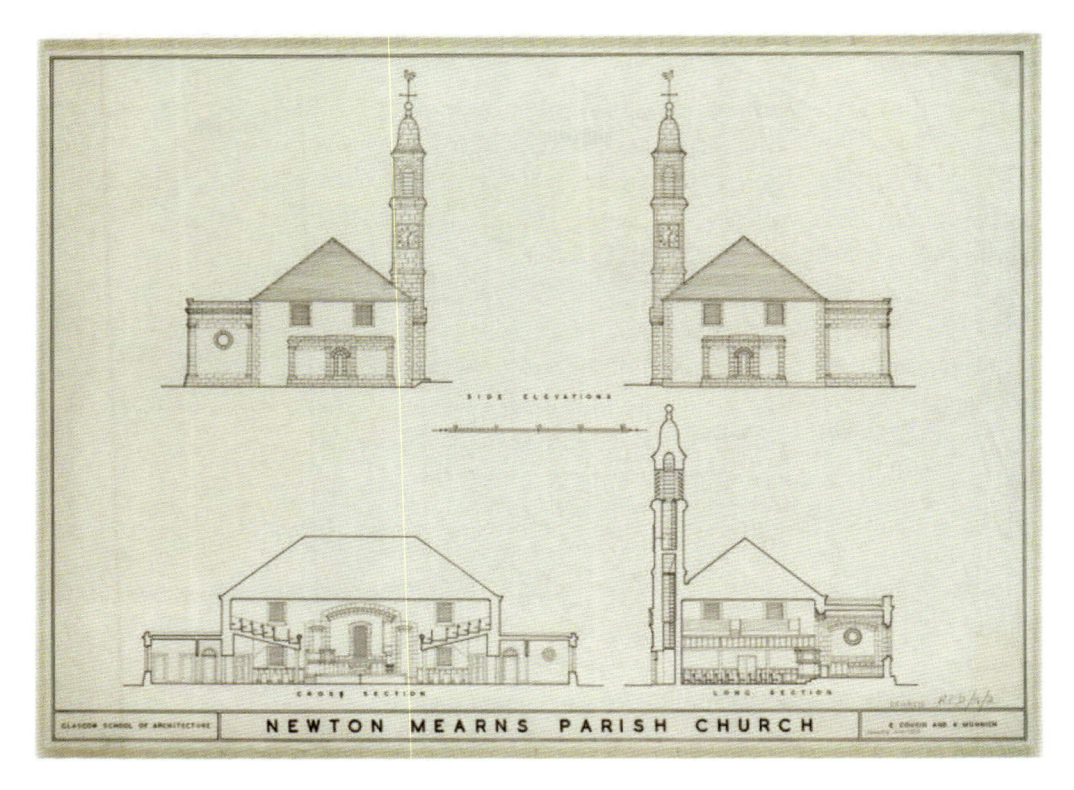

Cross sectional view of the proposed alterations to the church.

There are no pictures of the renovations being carried out. The previous booklet describes the old interior of the church as dark oak wood with the pews being boxes, some with tables. In order then to reconcile the discrepancies with the increase in number of sittings that the building seems to have had, it can only be that there was a re-organisation of the sittings at various times during the mid-19th century. In conclusion then I think that parts of the building are in fact much older with parts of the east and west walls and the door entrances being surviving remnants from an earlier time.

The part remaining to be discussed is the current clock tower. I have deliberately left it until last because I believe that the tower has been substantially rebuilt probably during the 1813 renovations. I think that a spire would have looked better, but there again, this was post reformation Scotland and a clock tower instead of a spire may have been considered more useful to better regulate the working day.

The Mearns Kirk Building - Past and Present

Exterior Markings and Features

The exterior of the church has a couple of noteworthy features, the most obscure one and an historically significant mark is probably overlooked as a mason's mark. It is on the side of the tower, and has to do with early mapping of the district. No, I hear you cry, not more obscure maps! Rest easy - this one is well known.

Early Ordinance Survey Mark 
The mark above is on the east side of the tower. It was used as a known height for the first Ordinance Board survey maps of the 1850s, and is part of the first levelling calculations of the country for mapping purposes.

The second interesting feature is the angel window frame on the north wall outside of the chancel window. Most people will walk past this and never think to look up at this sculptural treasure. I have checked the session records to find out if the sculptor is known but there is no reference made.

The keystone with the cross underneath the Angel window shows the location of the 1932 time capsule which is said to contain newspapers and coinage of the time.

The inscription on the windowsill below reads 'Omnia Nihil Praeter Deum' 'All nothing but God'. It is not known if this is a fragment from a larger sentence but in any case proves the theory of reuse of stonework from the older building.

The Mearns Kirk Building - Past and Present

The interior of the church has been altered since the 1932 renovations. In 2000, as part of a Millennium Project within the church, a new entrance door was created in what used to be the vestry, and the chancel floor was extended into the nave of the church which meant the removal of the first two rows of pews.

In 2005, the pews in the corner under the west gallery (beside the pulpit) were replaced with individual upholstered chairs to create a more flexible, multi-purpose area.

Author's Notes

1. Architectural drawings from the Royal Commission on the Ancient and Historical Monuments of Scotland.

2. Mearns Parish Kirk; Kirk Session Minutes 4 November 1927.

   Colour Images from the interior and exterior of the church in this chapter were taken by Mr T Harrison, Mr J Hamilton and Dr D Kidd. The black and white image of the church from 1890, by courtesy of Mr G Wilson. Hand drawn illustration by the author.

   Images of Greenbank House and Pollok House are from the Internet from their respective websites.

Stained Glass Windows

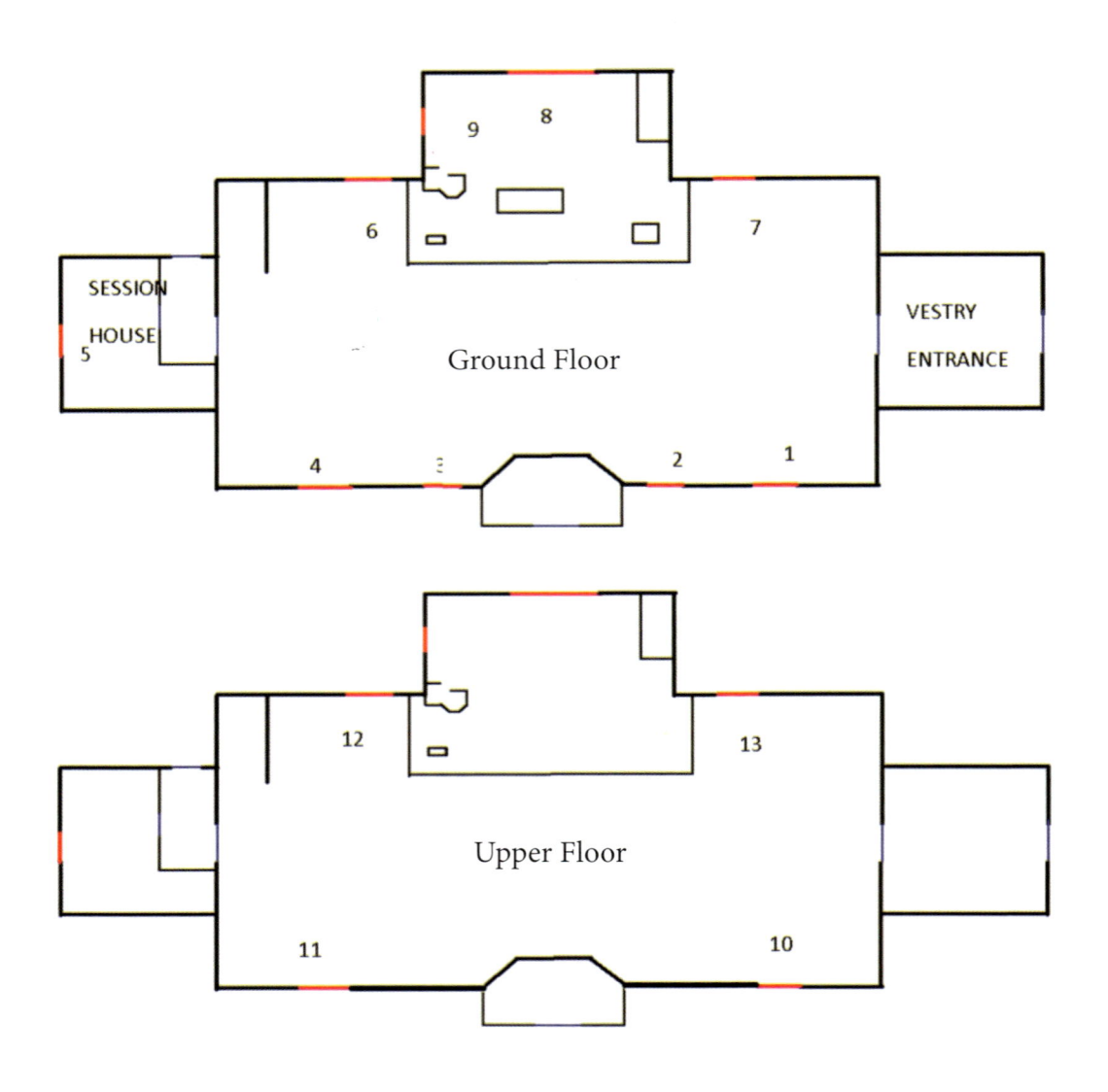

Ground Floor

SESSION HOUSE
VESTRY ENTRANCE

Upper Floor

Legend
Doors- Blue
Windows - Red

Floor Plan for Mearns Kirk Windows

Chapter Four: Part 1

Stained Glass Windows

All of the stained glass windows in the church building are a recent development dating from the 1930's. Prior to this the church was very plain and had no stained glass at all, which is surprising given the established patronage of the church by wealthy members of the congregation. There again, perhaps the idea of stained glass in the building was just too Catholic for some.

The stained glass windows that are in the church are of a high standard and quality. One of the main stained glass artists, with several examples of his work in the building, was Gordon McWhirter Webster (1908-1987).

Webster was a prolific artist working on numerous commissions for the Church of Scotland through the years. His work is the subject of a book in 2002 by Thomas M Honey, entitled *'Stained Glass Windows of Gordon Webster'* covering his work throughout Scotland, some of which, like the main chancel window, are quite exquisite in their composition and execution. He has been the subject of some articles regarding his work at St. Andrews University, and other places around the world. A quick Google check of his name will show just how prolific he was. A few examples of his work are also located nearby in Giffnock Parish Church.

This chapter follows the format established by the current booklet on the stained glass windows, using the sequence already established and adding detailed high resolution colour images of the windows together with close ups of the important details.

The major elements of the interior such as the Communion Table, Baptismal Font and Pulpit will receive similar treatment, all with high resolution images accompanying the text.

Stained Glass Windows

Stained Glass Windows

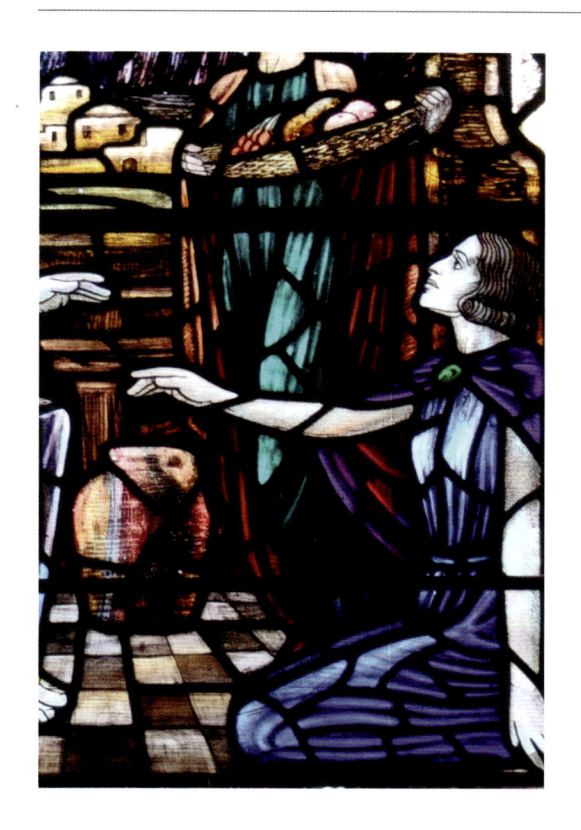

GROUND FLOOR

**Window No 1
Jesus, Martha and Mary in the House at Bethany**

This window is the memorial to Edith Hart, Wife of Rev. A. Drummond Duff who was minister at Mearnskirk from 1928 to 1951. The window is dated 11 February 1937, the date of her death. The window was designed by Gordon Webster.

The scene depicts Martha serving fruit and Mary with the jar of ointment used to anoint Jesus' feet. The houses of Bethany form the background.

To the Glory of God and in loving remembrance of Edith Hart, wife of the Rev. A. Drummond Duff, M.A. Minister of the Parish. obiit 11th February 1937.

Stained Glass Windows

Window No 2
St. Andrew's window

Stained Glass Windows

I make no apology for using full plates for this magnificent window. It was the gift of the children of the congregation to the church in 1932 and depicts St. Andrew Patron Saint of Scotland.

St Andrew is shown standing with his right hand raised and a piece of tartan in the style of a fishing net in his left hand. His robe is blue, with a scarlet lining symbolising sacrifice and behind him is the Saltire Cross on which he was martyred.

In the small panel above is the angel with the flaming sword, barring the gate of Eden to Adam and Eve, who crouch below. On the scroll is the text *'To him that overcommeth I will give to eat of the tree of life'* (Revelation 2:7)

Above the Angel on the border is a shield on which are two fishes, the emblem of St Andrew. The Celtic border is composed of thorn, a symbol of life.

Stained Glass Windows

**Window No 3
St Margaret's Window**

Stained Glass Windows

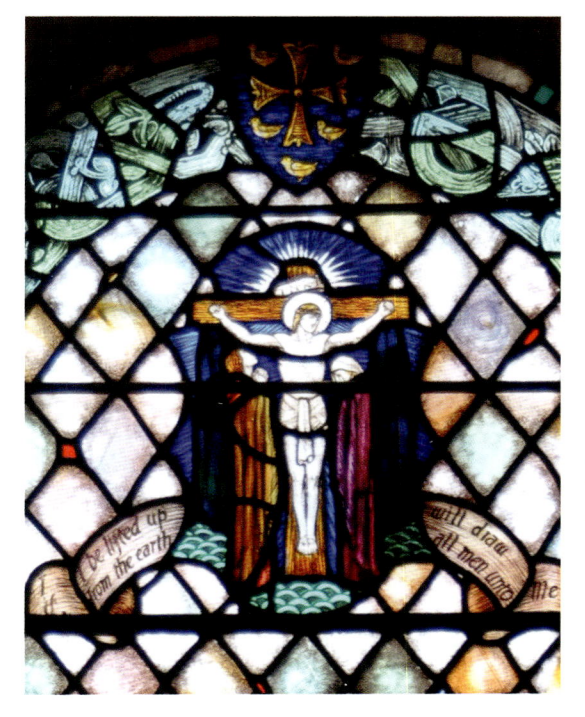

This window shows St. Margaret, Patron Saint of the Church of Scotland.

She is shown here holding in her left hand a censer, from which incense drifts upwards towards god, symbolising prayer. In her right hand she holds a bible, the symbol of truth.

In the lower part and shown behind her are two churches, the first below the censer is Celtic, the one below her right hand, Anglo Norman, symbolising the earlier church buildings on this site.

Above her flutter five birds which appear in her shield. In the small panel above is the crucified Christ, with Mary and John standing below. On the cross is the accusation INRI, Jesus of Nazareth King of the Jews.

On the scroll are the words *'I, if I be lifted up from the earth, will draw all men unto me'* (John 12:32)

The top element is the shield of St. Margaret, with the Cross and five swallows, hibernating birds, which symbolises resurrection.

The inscription at the bottom right reads *'To the Glory of God and in Memory of John and Margaret Strang. Gifted by William and Anne King of Malletsheugh'*

Stained Glass Windows

Window No 4
Parable of the Sower

and others fell upon good ground

To the Glory of God

In Loving Memory of Andrew Hamilton Gray and Elizabeth Brown McWilla[m]

Stained Glass Windows

This window was designed by James McPhee and was dedicated on 6 August 1967. The window is a memorial to Andrew Hamilton Gray and his wife Elizabeth Brown McMillan.

As well as illustrating the famous parable, the scene in this window also symbolises Communion, as the sower represents the bread of life, and the grapes represent the wine. Also visible is the dove of peace.

'*And others fell upon good ground*' was chosen as a fitting memorial of a life's work as a master miller.

Stained Glass Windows

Window No 8
The Chancel

The chancel window was designed by Gordon Webster and dedicated in 1931. The window is engraved 'To the glory of God and in loving memory of Agnes Fairley and George Ingram' It was gifted by their daughter Agnes. F. Henderson

The scene is from the Vision of St John in the Book of Revelation. The central figure is the Spiritual Christ. He is clad in a red robe gathered at the breast with a golden band. On His head is a crown and on His robe are Christian symbols embroidered in red and gold.

The following symbols can be seen; the Chi-Ro figure, the alpha and omega, the keys to Heaven and Hell.

Stained Glass Windows

The top element consists of seven figures holding seven vials, gifts of the Spirit: wisdom, counsel, understanding, might, knowledge, fear of the Lord and delight in the Lord.

Behind the central figure are seven candles that rise from the throne, around whose flames are a great arc of Light. Light comes from the head of Christ, and beyond Him are seven stars.

Stained Glass Windows

On the throne depicted here are the faces of the four main beasts, man, the lion, the ox and the eagle. Beneath his feet are shown clouds, and the rainbow over the sea of glass. In the lower right hand corner is the Lamb triumphant standing on the book with the seven seals, symbols of the Last Judgement.

The figure in the lower left is St. John depicted as a pilgrim. He is kneeling, gazing upwards at the Vision. He wears a soft brown robe symbolising the earth and carries a bag and a water bottle. In his belt is a hammer which he would have used to break up stones during his exile on Patmos.

Stained Glass Windows

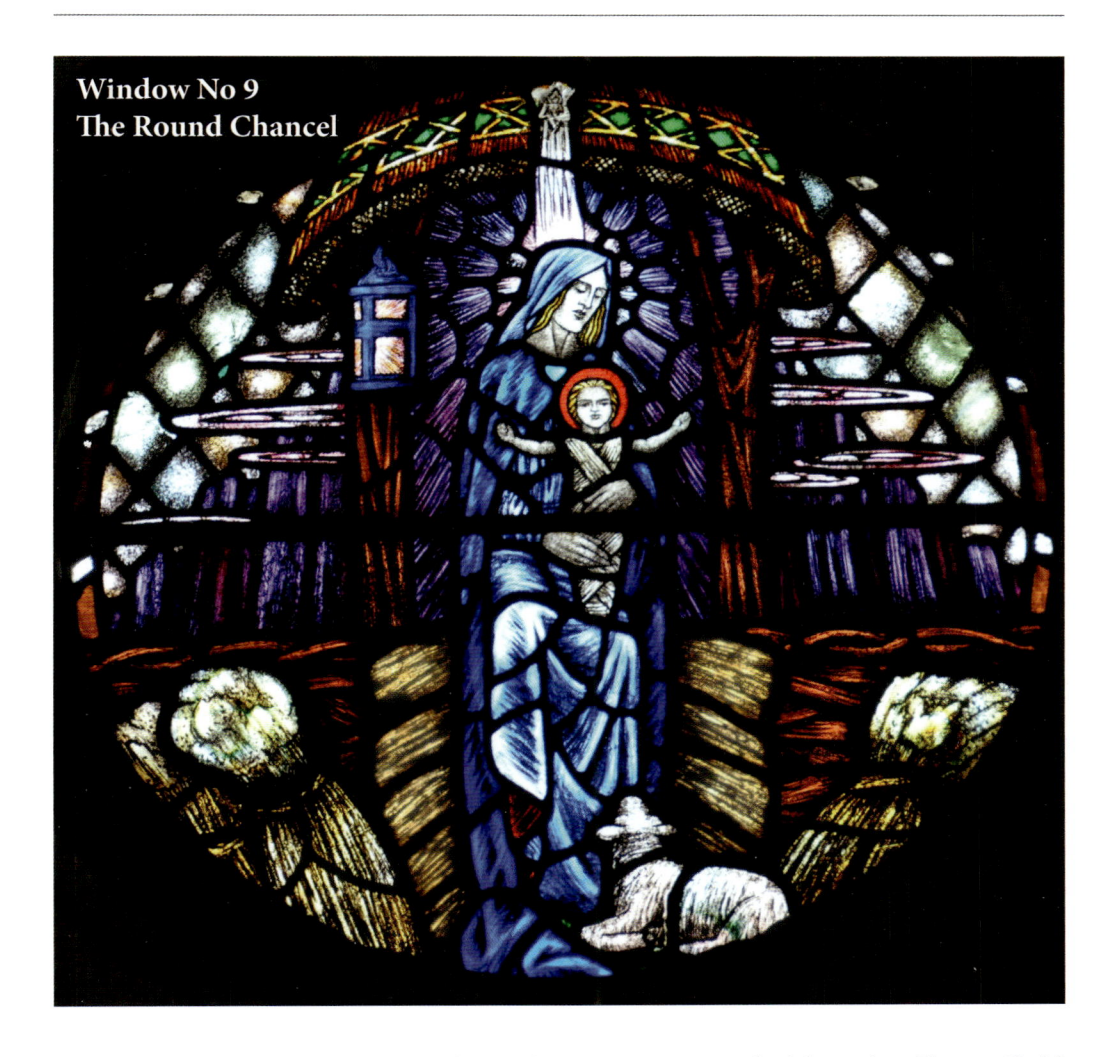

**Window No 9
The Round Chancel**

The subject here is treated simply. In the centre is Mary holding the Christ Child with his arms outstretched, around whose head is a scarlet halo. Above Mary's head comes radiance from a star which illuminates the scene and merges into the purple of the mountains in the background, and symbolises divine guidance.

Mary stands within a thatched roofed structure, reminiscent of the birth of Christ, a lantern lights the left hand side of the image and below are sheaves of wheat leaning against wicker fencing. At Mary's feet is a lamb looking up at the child in her arms.

This window was designed by Gordon Webster and dedicated in 1931. It was a gift to the church from Mrs Duff erected in memory of their only child.

Stained Glass Windows

Window No 6
St Francis of Assisi

SAINT FRANCIS ENCOUNTERS THE THREE MAIDENS POVERTY, CHASTITY, OBEDIENCE

Stained Glass Windows

This window was designed by Gordon Webster in 1960 and depicts the scene of St. Francis meeting three maidens.

These maidens are the rule on which the Franciscan Order and that of the Poor Sisters of St. Claire are founded, namely poverty, chastity and obedience

The composition of this window compared with that on the opposite wall which dated from the 1930's shows how much the artist has improved his technique over the years. The figures are clearly executed and the composition of the window fits neatly with the life of one of the most loved saints.

The artist's signature and date is visible on the lower right of the window just above the border.

The window is a memorial to the life of Lucinda Gamble French (22 Sept 1889 - 31 Jan 1958)

The buildings in the background have a distinctly medieval Italian look to them representing the Saint's home town of Assisi.

Stained Glass Windows

Window No 10
Suffer the little children to come unto me

Stained Glass Windows

This window was designed by James McPhie and made by Douglas Strachan in 1932.

The scene is from the Life of Jesus which is told in at least three gospels of the New Testament; Matthew 19:14, Luke 18:16 and Mark 10:4 showing Jesus receiving children from their mothers and blessing them.

Compare the expressions on the faces of the mothers and children with those of the two disciples standing in the background behind Jesus. They do not look happy at this occasion.

Compare this window with the other story windows on the ground floor and you will see that this one is the first that does not show Jesus as the central figure, the mother and child are the focus here, with Christ positioned off to the right.

The window was dedicated in 1933 and is the memorial for Mary Stuart Bow, wife of William Symington Davie, who died on 11 November 1932.

Stained Glass Windows

First Floor Windows
Window No 11
The Pathway

Stained Glass Windows

The window was commissioned by Sheena McMurtrie in memory of her parents, Jessie and Terry. The window reflects their commitment to the Christian faith and their main interests. It was designed and manufactured by Catriona R. MacKinnon, and was dedicated by the Rev Joe Kavanagh on August 21 2005.

The central focus is Jesus, Light of the World, and from this emanates three intertwined non uniform circles. The higher blue circle represents spiritual life, the central blue/green circle represents the seasons, with natural features including trees, flower and the produce of the fields. The lower pink circle portrays community life, with illustrations of local buildings, such as Holmwood House, Mearns Kirk and the old Main Street of Newton Mearns.

Weaving its way through all these areas and depicted in purple is the 'path of life' with bends and twists reflecting the ups and downs of life.

Stained Glass Windows

Window No 12
The British Legion Memorial

Stained Glass Windows

The Newton Mearns Branch of the Royal British Legion was formed in the church halls on 29 January 1946. This window was designed and manufactured by Catriona R. MacKinnon of Ayr to commemorate the golden jubilee of the Branch and was dedicated on 9 June 1996. The window was commissioned by Alan Groom, the Branch President, but following his death in 1997 the window also stands as a memorial to him in recognition of his work for the Branch.

The main features of the window are the crest of the Royal British Legion with the dates 1946-1996 and motifs such as the fish of St Andrew, the Church of Mearns Kirk, a Celtic cross, wheat and grapes, symbolising the communion elements, a Scottish thistle, the Greek letters alpha and omega, reminders of God's eternal presence, and further Greek letters IHS symbolising Christ.

On the left of the legion crest in evening shades of purple and orange the sun sets over hills and lochs. High in the evening sky are two eagles, traditional symbols of the services and the Church. On the right of the crest is the sun rising in the morning, with rays in subtle hues of pink, yellow and orange that emanate outwards and upwards towards enlightenment and resurrection.

Central to this part of the window are the badges of the Services: Royal Navy, Army and Royal Air Force, together with an outline of the parish boundary showing Mearns Kirk in its correct place within the boundary, signifying the Legion's long association with the church. At the end of the path to the church is a bugle calling us to worship.

Scattered through the window are seven small blue and red spots of colour, showing the ecumenical spirit in which the window was conceived. The laurel and oak motifs on the border are taken from the Royal Army Chaplain's department badge and symbolise strength and victory.

The epitaph that appears in the top and bottom halves of the window are taken from verse four of Lawrence Binyon's poem *'For the Fallen'* published in September 1914:

> *They shall not grow old as we that are left grow old*
> *Age shall not weary them nor, the years condemn.*
> *At the setting of the sun and in the morning,*
> *We shall remember them.*

Stained Glass Windows

Window No 13
Eastwood District Council

Stained Glass Windows

The window was commissioned to commemorate the lifetime of Eastwood District Council from 1974 to 1996. The window was designed and manufactured by Catriona R. MacKinnon of Ayr, and was dedicated by the Rev. Roderick Campbell on 9 June 1996.

Central to the window is the crest of Eastwood District council. This is superimposed on a boundary plan of Eastwood District in green with a heavy lead outline. The leaf border features many of the trees of the area including oak, sycamore, chestnut, beech, birch, holly and willow. Each of the four corners represents developments in the fields of music, sport, drama and education.

Many of the area's features are shown in their correct positions on the plan, at the top of the window being the listed Thornliebank School, with the bridge and the waterfall at Rouken Glen immediately below it. Clockwise from this is the viaduct at Busby over the river Cart, the 14th century Mearns Castle, the conservation village of Eaglesham, the wind turbine development at Drumduff Hill, the cotton factory building and loch at Netherplace, the Brother Loch, Black Loch, White Loch, Little Loch, Long Loch all noted for fishing, the monument to Robert Pollok on the A77 at Eastwood Golf Course and Duncarnock Hill, the site of an iron age hill fort.

In addition there is a flag denoting the district's many golf courses, pine trees representing forestry and tree planting and deciduous trees representing conservation and tree protection. Sheep and a sheaf of corn mark the long history with farming in the district, together with wood sorrel and butterbur, two of the many wild flowers in Rouken Glen Park.

Near the centre of the plan is the crest of the unicorn, taken from above the doorway of Eastwood House, the Council's meeting place from 1974-1982 prior to the opening of the Council Headquarters.

Finally, throughout the window are seven brightly coloured spots, the number seven being the Christian Symbol for the 'perfect number', so marking the installation of the window in an ecclesiastical building.

Stained Glass Windows

Window No 10
The Children's Window

All are Children of God

Far round the world

Thy children sing their song

GIFTED BY
NANCY AND NORMAN ANDERSON 1996

Stained Glass Windows

Commissioned by Church Members Nancy and Norman Anderson and designed and manufactured by Catriona R. MacKinnon, the window was dedicated by Rev Roderick Campbell on 22 December 1996. It illustrated the theme that we are 'All Children of God'

The lines of text in the Window are taken from the first lines of the following hymns; Basil Mathews (1879-1951) *'Far round the world they children sing thy song'* and John W Chadwick's (1840-1904) *'Eternal ruler of the ceaseless round of circling planets singing on their way'*.

The five children represent the five continents of our planet and between them a sense of caring and sharing is portrayed. Music, happiness, fun and an awareness of nature and animals is shown in flowers, fields, a tractor, birds, a pet dog and a fish in a stream. Stepping stones in the water represent the bridging between peoples and of forging links, which is also depicted in the boat mooring. The boat mooring represents safety, security and bonding.

The sense of communication and sharing is continued through circles and spheres, the bicycle wheels, the wheelchair, a skipping rope and in the top right a boomerang which circles and returns. There is also a spinning top or a circling planet. The part border of bubbles or balloons creates a sense of rising with the sun, giving a feeling of warmth and light. The circles throughout the window signify the love and care which should surround us all.

Ceremonial Furniture

Chapter Four: Part 2

Ceremonial Furniture

Ceremonial Furniture

The second half of this chapter deals with the main fixtures and fittings of the church, such as the organ, communion table and pulpit together with any art works that are part of the church interior. Colour photographs are used and a short monograph provides their history.

The Pulpit

The oak pulpit was presented by Miss Fergusson-Pollok in 1932 in memory of the Pollok family. The carving on its central panel is a Celtic cross and the Pollok family crest appears on the end panel. Thistles, symbolic of Christ's suffering and of Scotland, surround the cross and form the base of the reading lamp. The soaring eagle on the corner of the pulpit symbolises Christ's ascension

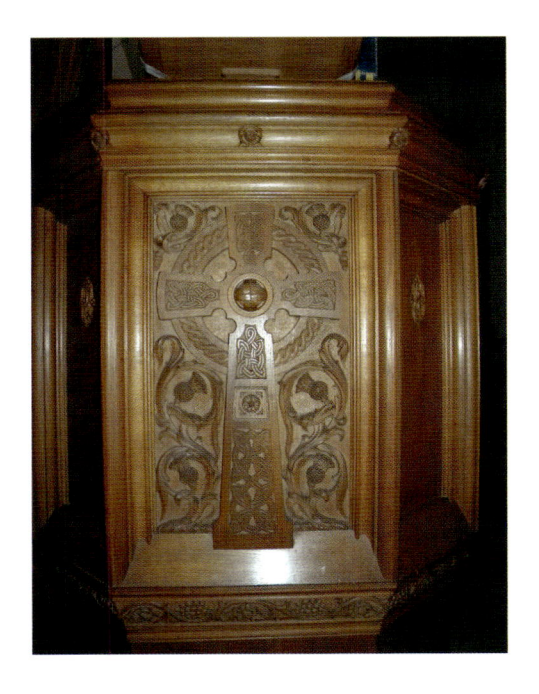

Ceremonial Furniture

Ceremonial Furniture

The Baptismal Font

The baptismal font was presented to the church in 1932 as a memorial to William Maver who had been an elder of the church for twenty one years. This is commemorated in the carvings on the cover.

The font also contains carvings of the lamb, symbolic of Christ and a pelican, symbolic of Christ's love, because during a famine the adult pelican will pierce its own breast to feed its young on its own blood.

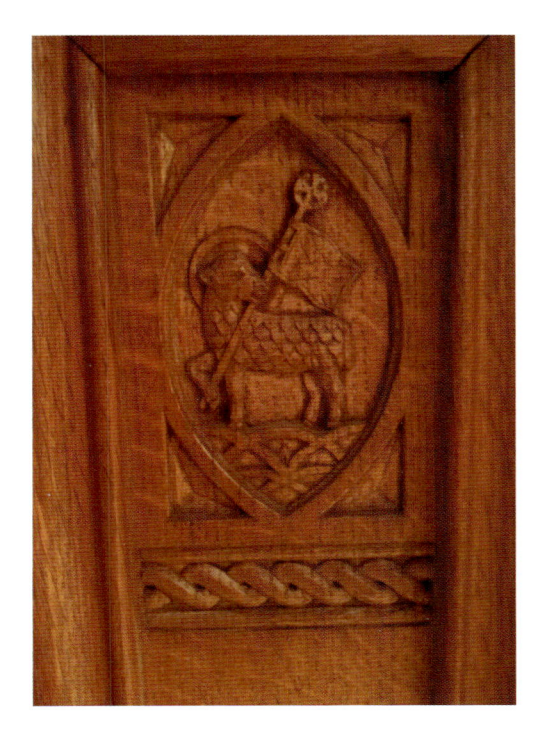

Ceremonial Furniture

The Communion Table

The communion table was a gift to the congregation on the centenary of the building in April 1913, by the Women's Guild. When it was made together with the chair it cost £52.00. The table was designed by Mr P. Macgregor Chalmers of Glasgow and made by Messrs McKay of Bothwell Street, Glasgow.

Below the top leaf of the table is a frieze of carved grapes and vine leaves. The table top rests on two fluted Doric pillars and the central span has the words **'This Do In Remembrance of Me'** from either the Gospel of Luke 22:19 or 1st Corinthians 11:24 which commemorates the Last Supper.

The central panel contains a roundel of vines bound with leaves containing the letters I H S from the Latin, meaning 'Jesus Hominum Salvator, Jesus the Saviour of Men'; the border consists of ornately carved oak leaves.

Ceremonial Furniture

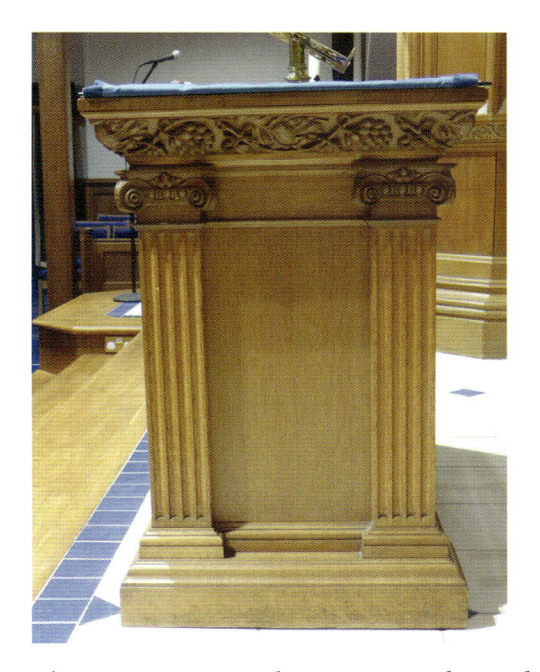

The communion chair was made at the same time as the communion table, matching the Doric pillar design, and bears the name of the church.

The side panel of the organ in the choir echoes the central motif of the pulpit and the alpha and omega symbols are echoed in the central figure in the main stained glass window in the chancel.

Ceremonial Furniture

The Lectern Tapestry

The lectern shown here was made by former fabric convenor Duncan Campbell in 1982 from two oak bench pews taken from the old church hall. It was made at the machine shop at Govan Shipyard where Duncan worked. The cross on the front is a copy of the pulpit cross along with two thistles that echo those found elsewhere in the interior and in the stained glass windows. From the remaining wood Duncan also made handles for the collection bags.

The lectern is dedicated to the memory of Kate Ritchie, an elder of the kirk.

The tapestry of St. Ninian and the lectern fall were both made by congregation member Audrey Blair. The symbolism of the lectern fall echoes many elements of the stained glass and communion furniture within the building and is an impressive work.

Ceremonial Furniture

Ceremonial Furniture

The Organ

When the church re-opened in 1932 after the substantial renovations, a 'new' pipe organ was installed in the newly created chancel extension. It came from the Glasgow City Hall and was almost 100 years old when installed in 1932. So it was not surprising, then, that the Session were advised at the end of 1981 that, despite a major overhaul some 5 years earlier, it was approaching the end of its life and would need to be replaced.

The Session decided to mark the Golden Jubilee of the renovations of the church with a new organ and an appeal for funds was launched by Rev. Roderick Campbell in spring 1982. By the summer 1982 enough funds were raised and with the consultation of John Turner, the organist of Glasgow Cathedral and the Mearns Kirk organist and choirmaster A.J. MacPherson a new organ was built and installed by Rushworth and Dreaper before the end of 1982.

Some parts of the old organ were retained, as was the fine light oak case which houses the organ.

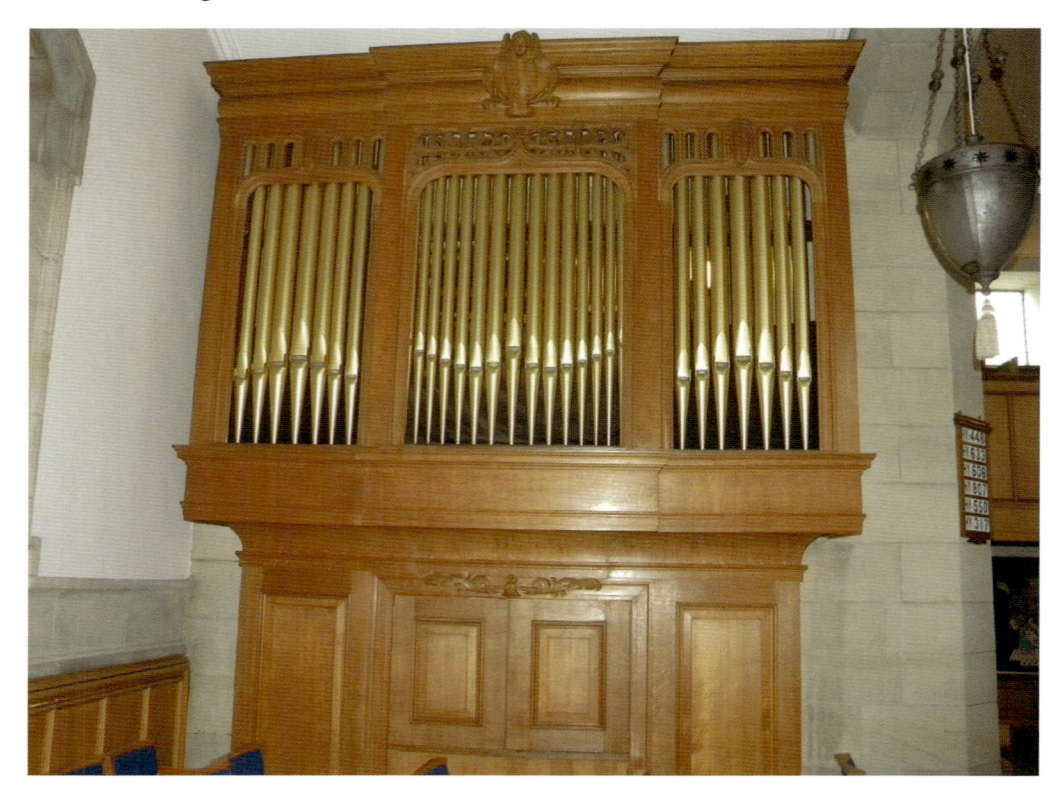

Ceremonial Furniture

The Tapestry of St. Ninian

St. Ninian, the bringer of Christianity to Scotland in the fourth Century AD is celebrated here.

The central stylised motifs of his robe are based on the eternal knot pattern. Here four eternal knots are used and the design originates from the Book of Kells and shows the religious links with Ireland in the early Catholic Church.

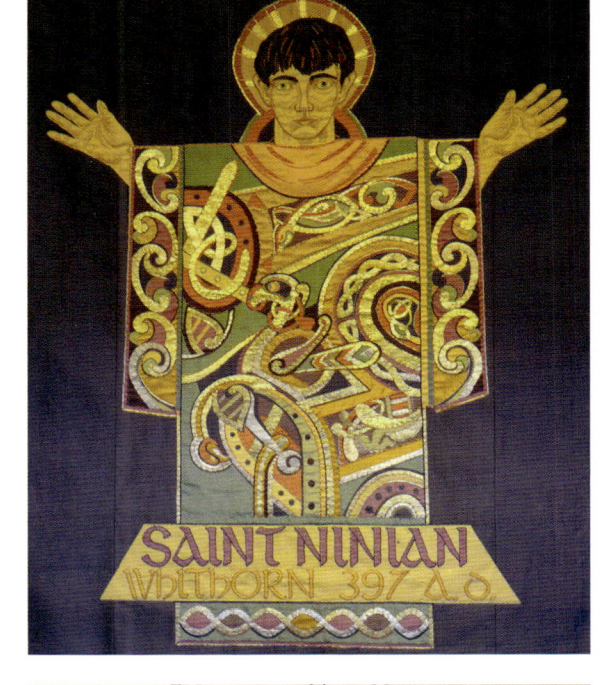

The Eternal Flame

The lamp of the eternal flame used to hang in the chancel above the communion table as can be seen in previous views of the church interior.

The lamp was a gift to the church by the Hart family in memory of Edith Duff nee' Hart, wife of the Minister Alfred Drummond Duff.

Prior to electricity arriving in the 1940s, the lamp had a bad habit of smoking during the sermon causing the beadle regularly to extinguish it.

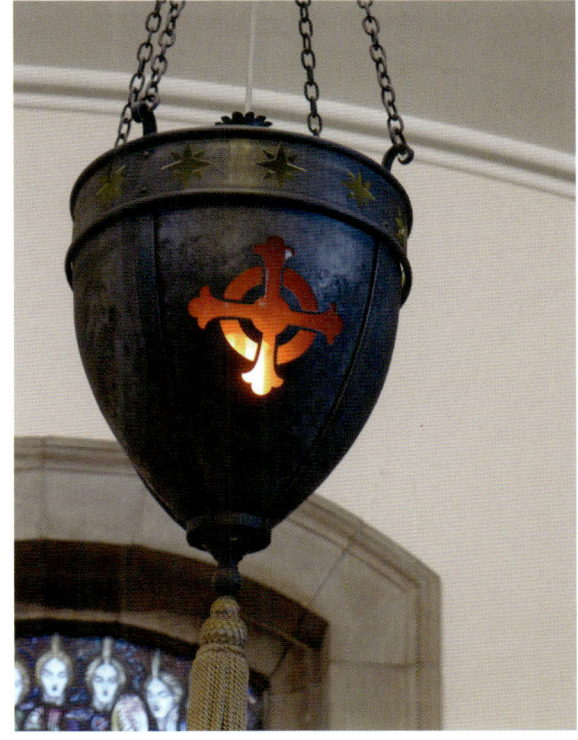

Ceremonial Furniture

Lord Goold Commemorative Tapestry

Ceremonial Furniture

Lord Goold Commemorative Tapestry

The commemorative tapestry shown opposite was presented to Mearns Kirk on 19 September 1992 by Lord Goold in memory of his late wife Sheena. It was designed by James J More of the Edinburgh Tapestry Company Ltd following discussions with Lord Goold and Rev. Roderick Campbell. Lord Goold was an elder of the Kirk and Lord Lieutenant of Renfrewshire.

The design of the tapestry is based on a series of ascending curves which lead the eye upwards and which are formed from the river of life, the path of life and the tree of life and the corona surrounding the trinity. The path, the tree and the corona form the initial 'S', the top of which is left unenclosed.

The river of life contains the symbolic fish of Christianity swimming beneath the rock, which is Christ the sure foundation on which the church is built. The rock is also a stepping stone to the path of life which winds by the riverbank towards paradise, sometimes in light, sometimes in shade and sometimes glowing with the Holy Spirit. At times the path is rocky, at times smooth, but always strewn with symbols including the alpha and omega, the first and last Greek letters which remind us that God is with us from beginning to end; the rising phoenix, the symbol of hope from despair; the Celtic cross of eternity; St. Andrew's Cross, in memory of Scotland's patron saint; and the key to open the gateway of heaven.

The rock shapes at the lower part of the path are suggestive of the hills of Arran, a favourite holiday destination of the Goold family.

Above the path is the tree of life below which flies the dove, symbol of peace and of the soul, and the butterfly, which emerges from the seemingly lifeless chrysalis so a symbol of the resurrection.

The field lilies, spring irises and daffodils are interspersed with thistles, an emblem of Mearns Kirk and ferns, symbolic of growth and renewal. Beyond the tree the Celtic cross glistens with its special blessing of eternal love, and adjacent are silhouettes of Mearns Kirk and Glasgow University Tower.

Yachts, symbolic of the church as a ship of faith venturing to sea, lead the vision upwards to paradise and the Celtic symbol of the trinity, set within the corona. the light of all light.

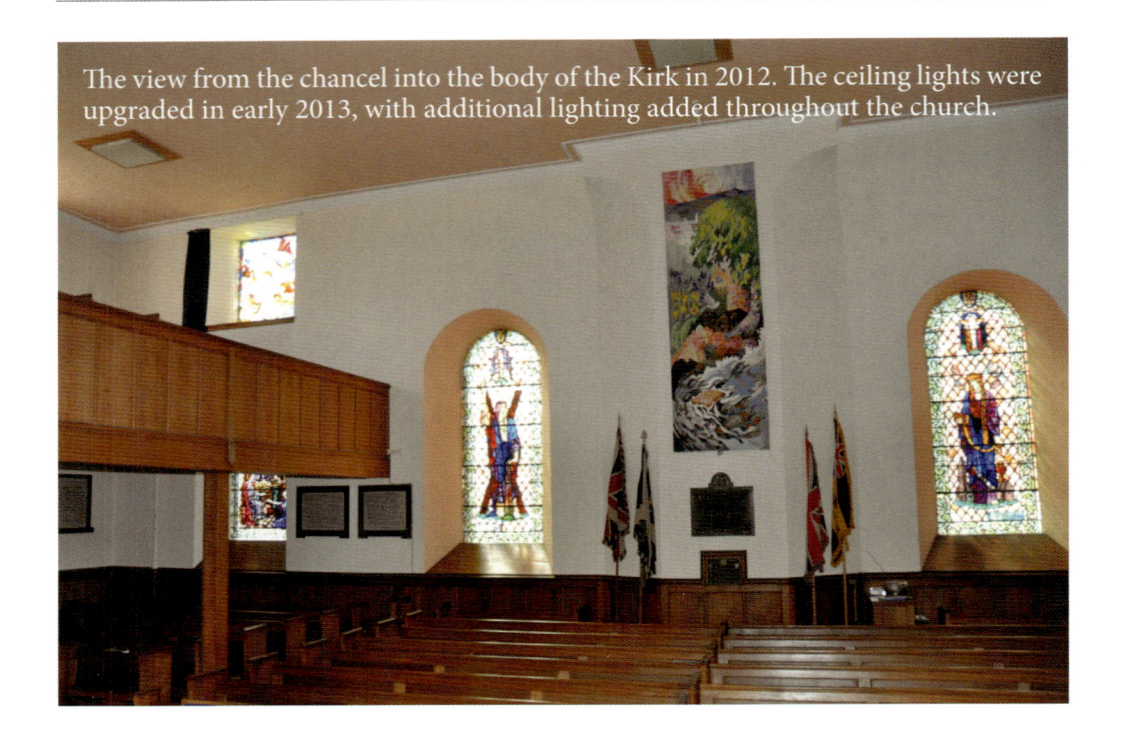

Ceremonial Furniture

The view from the chancel into the body of the Kirk in 2012. The ceiling lights were upgraded in early 2013, with additional lighting added throughout the church.

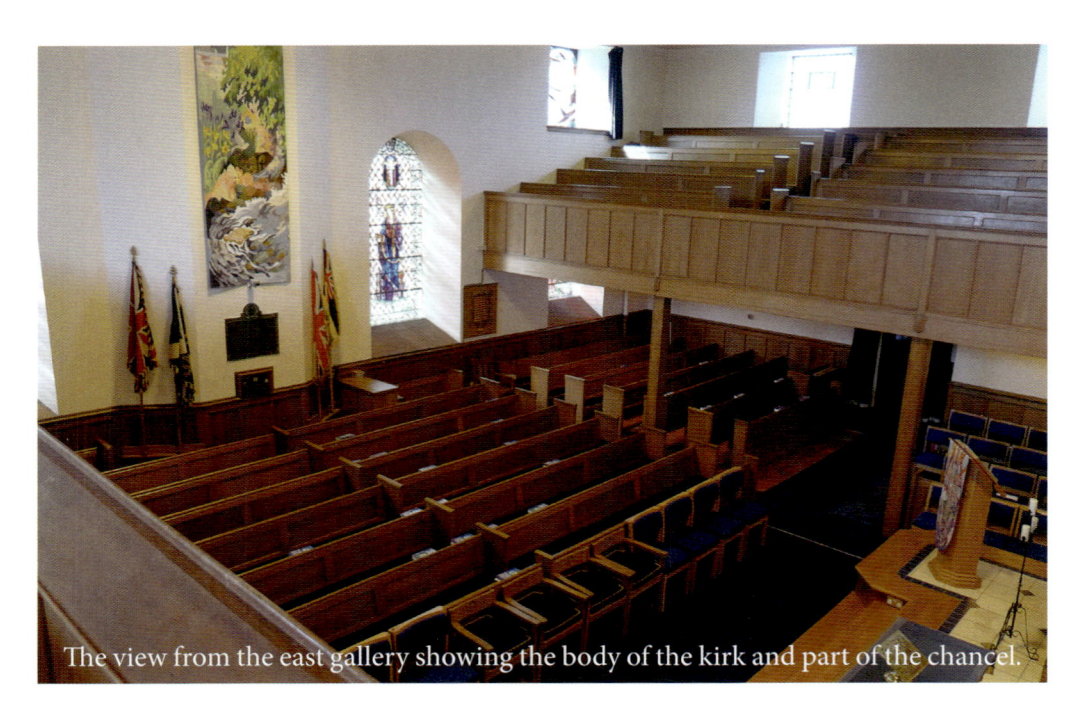

The view from the east gallery showing the body of the kirk and part of the chancel.

Ceremonial Furniture

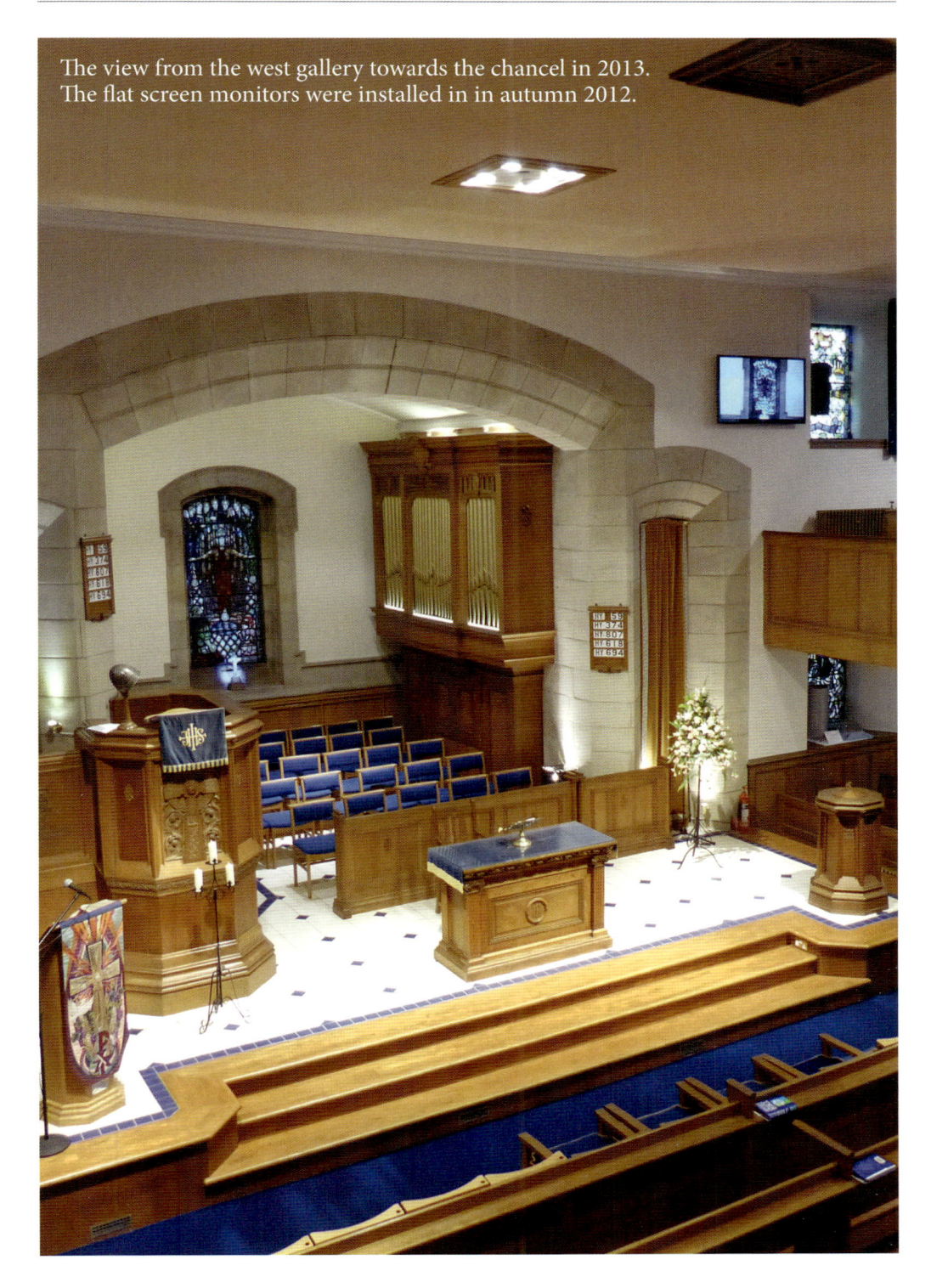

The view from the west gallery towards the chancel in 2013. The flat screen monitors were installed in in autumn 2012.

Ministers of Mearns - Past and Present

In 2000 the vestry was converted into an entrance hall and the window was replaced by the current entrance door.

Mearns Kirk. Picture taken from the Glebe in summer 2012

Chapter Five:

Ministers of Mearns Past and Present

Given that there has been a religious presence on this site for several centuries, I thought that it would be interesting from a historical point of view to see just how far the records would support the identification of those men who ministered here. To that end I have relied on the evidence supplied in previous publications and have tried as far as possible to check all details then published.

The outcome so far has been quite surprising and very promising, in that, as far as official church records go, and with suitable research at the library of University of Glasgow, it is possible to give the names and dates of appointment and either death or removal from the parish for most if not all of the ministers since the Reformation. What is even more surprising is that there were a few ministers that were local men from well-known local families of this area.

I thought that I would endeavour to provide readers with a biographical record and if possible an image of those that have ministered here in the last one hundred and fifty years. For those that came before the invention of photography, the biographical information attached to each name will have to suffice as no known images exist. I have decided that what follows here should be in reverse chronological order, to give the readers a chance to familiarise themselves with those staff members and ministers that may still be around.[1]

It seems only right that the governing body of the church is included here. To that end I have included as much information about the current and previous Kirk Session members that is available. It was decided that a photograph of the current Kirk Session was required, and it was taken in 2012. The intention is to provide as complete and accurate picture of the organisation of Mearns Kirk as is possible.

---

[1] Biographical information comes from the Kirk session records in the National Archives of Scotland and the Church of Scotland publications ' Fasti Ecclesiae Scoticanae' Synod of Glasgow and Synod of Paisley' vols.3,8,9

Ministers of Mearns - Past and Present

Rev. Joe Kavanagh   1998 - present

The current minister of Means Kirk is the living embodiment that the Lord moves in mysterious ways his wonders to perform, because no one who knew Joe Kavanagh in his early life could have predicted he would become a Church of Scotland pastor.

Joe, born on January 27, 1957, outlined the byways that took him from his early life in Johnstone to Newton Means: "I was born into the Catholic faith and kept going until I was about 15 and then decided, as teenagers often do whatever denomination they belong to, that it was time to swan off, so I went nowhere.

"It wasn't a conscious decision to leave for another denomination, I just stopped going to Church. Then when I was about 21, I became friendly with a family who were involved in the Baptist Church and I was part of that denomination until I was 29 when I left and joined the Church of Scotland, as a member of Johnstone High."

Educated at St. Margaret's Primary in Johnstone and St. Mirin's Academy in Paisley he started university life at St. Andrews on a five-year course the Church laid down he had to undertake. It involved a four year honours course, and he obtained a first-class degree in ecclesiastical history and a diploma in pastoral theology. He later became a graduate of both Edinburgh and Glasgow Universities, with Master of Theology degrees from both of them.

After leaving St. Andrews he served a probationary period at Wormit and Balmerino in Fife, was ordained in 1992 as minister of Girvan High and in 1998 he was appointed to Means Kirk.

Ministers of Mearns - Past and Present

In the years between leaving school and entering university he had a variety of jobs, starting in the Trustee Savings Bank then in the accounts office of Balfour Kilpatrick, a fitter's mate at the Royal Ordnance Factory at Bishopton and then on the factory floor of the giant Linwood car factory graduating to the office before it's closure.

Now he believes it's a help to his ministry that he knows of life outside the confines of the pulpit: "For me that's always been a plus. I was an ordinary person, so to speak, and had been in jobs to know what life was like and it has always kept me grounded."

After the close of Linwood he came to a crossroads: "It was a case of what do I do now, and because I was quite heavily involved in the Baptist Church I began to think of full-time Christian service." He went to college at the Bible Training Institute, then situated in the west end of Glasgow in the building currently housing the arts and entertainment complex, Oran Mor, as he observes: "A different type of spirit altogether.

"I was there for three years and I worked with my local church and tried to understand what the next big step should be for me. It turned out to be the Church of Scotland, and the reason was that doors didn't really open for me with the Baptists.

"I was assured there was a call waiting for me. My own minister thought that and so did the head of the Bible College, the Rev. Geoffrey Grogan who I respected very much. I just came to realise that the Church of Scotland was for me, so I went there, which was a big step for me."

However, he failed in his first attempt to win selection for the ministry: "The letter said they weren't going to accept me for the present, but I was encouraged to immerse myself in the life of my local congregation. They were almost saying not yet, rather than a big no".

How did his family and friends accept him switching from the Catholic faith? "I suppose some folks found it difficult to understand because I came from a well established Catholic family. My mother was the organist in St. Margaret's Church for 25 years, my father ran the football team and the Scout troop linked to the chapel.

Ministers of Mearns - Past and Present

Rev. Joe Kavanagh with the Right Rev. Albert Bogle, Moderator of the General Assembly, dedicating a commemorative plaque marking the 200th anniversary of the church building on the 19th February 2013

"For my parents the Baptist Church was a bit of an enigma to them but the Church of Scotland was mainstream so it was perhaps more acceptable and my Dad became very proud of me. My twin brother went to South Africa and he became quite high up in the Masons.

"People would meet my Dad and would ask him how the twins were doing. He would reply as a bit of fun: "Oh, Tom is in South Africa and a big shot in the Masons and Joe is a Minister in the Church of Scotland.""

He outlined his aims for his ministry at Mearns: "To be there for people, to be their pastor and hopefully they can come and talk to me about all sorts of issues in life. Of course to preach from the Bible which is very much part of the Church of Scotland ethos – I'm very committed to that. And whether it's in the Church or the parish, to make known God's love in ways that people come to see themselves precious in God's eyes."

He smiled as he recalled one of his highlights in recent years, away from the Church, when as a Celtic supporter he revealed his pleasure at playing on their ground: "I captained a ministers' team against a side made up of politicians in a charity game at Celtic Park, and we won."

Written by Rodger Baillie, a church member and journalist who interviewed Joe in Sept. 2012.

Ministers of Mearns - Past and Present

Roderick D. M. Campbell   1979 – 1997

Roderick Campbell was born in Glasgow on 1 August 1943, the son of Thomas Campbell and Francis McKenzie. Despite being a son of the Manse, The Church of Scotland Ministry was not Roderick's first career choice. He trained as a technical teacher in Glasgow and taught in Glasgow, with VSO in Tanzania and then in London.

After London he returned to Scotland to study at the University of Edinburgh, from where he received his Bachelor of Divinity in 1974. He was approached by the Board of World Mission for service at Nairobi, Kenya. His first parish was Nairobi's St. Andrews, Presbyterian Church of East Africa. There he met Sue, his wife. Together they have two daughters, Catriona and Sheona, who were born after he and Sue moved to Mearns Kirk. He was inducted at Mearns Kirk on 1 June 1979 and stayed until 30 September 1997.

In 1997 he was asked by the Secretary of State to be chair of the Victoria NHS Trust in Glasgow and at which point he left the ministry as the two could not be done together effectively.

At the end of 1999 he went to Sudan with the Church of Scotland Overseas Council, training people to rebuild their lives and communities.

In 2003 he returned to Scotland, to be the Minister at the Parish Church of St. Andrew and St. George in Edinburgh. He is currently Minister at Appin and Lismore Parish Churches where he was inducted on 30th August 2008.

Roderick has been on the board of various associations and organisations, the Glasgow Lodging House Mission, National Church Extension, Greater Glasgow Drug Action Team to name but a few. He was also a keen member of the Territorial Army and while at Mearns Kirk was a regular broadcaster on Radio Clyde and Radio Scotland.

Roderick drove HGV trucks filled with aid to refugee camps in war-torn former Yugoslavia.

In 1994 following a visit to war-torn Croatia he initiated a charity to help refugees from the former Yugoslavia. The Mearns Kirk Aid 'Reach Out' charity organised by volunteers from the church collected aid and medical supplies involving local businesses, schools and churches in the area, delivering tons of materials over a duration of 3 years to Croatia. Roderick personally drove HGV trucks on several occasions delivering to hospitals and refugee camps out there.

He has three publications credited to him, the first published privately on 'Kirk and Party' (1988) and 'Challenge to Change' University of St Andrews Press (1997), 'Four Pillars', Doctoral Thesis, Pittsburgh TS 2008.

and would like to thank everyone in the district who has supported us including the schools and the churches."

Rev Roderick Campbell and charity workers, Ginty Greer, Shelia Goldie, John and Betty Mcinnes and Stan Stirling surrounded by 300 boxes and 200 bags of aid.

Photograph: Don Clements

Ministers of Mearns - Past and Present

David Anderson Black   1960-1978

Memories of the Rev. David Anderson Black as recalled by David Arthur.

David Black was called to our church here at Mearnskirk from Partick Old in 1960.

At the age of 16, whilst attending a church service where David lived in Stepps, he recognised God's call upon his life to the Ministry. He began his training for the Ministry of the Baptist Church, graduating MA of Glasgow University.

During the Second World War he served King and Country as Chaplain to the Royal Marines. During this period of service he married Betty who was the mainstay of his life for so many years. At the cessation of war he decided to transfer to the Church of Scotland, the family moved to St. Andrew's, and the University from which he graduated BD in 1949.

In that same year, David was called to the Parish and charge of Ceres, Fife. A delightful village set amidst rich agricultural land. Here David exercised for the very first time, the very considerable gifts which he brought to the ministry. Life in Ceres was happy. Glenys had been born in Wales but the family now extended with the births of Martin, Alison and William.

In 1954 David accepted the call to be the minister of the parish and charge of Partick Old, in the very heart of the City of Glasgow. Situated at the foot of Byres Road, looking out onto the Western Infirmary, a stone's throw from the University, and surrounded by the tenements of Partick, David set to his new ministry with a will. Here he encountered the demands of a busy city parish and became acutely aware of its problems. Worship lay at the heart of the gospel and to that end he led his congregation to building a new chancel in the church. Worship and service, preaching and pasturing.

Ministers of Mearns - Past and Present

There was always more work to be undertaken. David became the Industrial Chaplain to the ship-building firm of WD & O Henderson, Chaplain to the Royal Navy Volunteer Reserve (Royal Marines). At this time David began a most important relationship with Dr Shenkin in the study of Pastoral Psychology.

I can well remember when David came amongst us. Our church was holding a garden fete in Mrs Brocklehurst's huge garden and lawns (just behind our church halls on Ayr Road). The fete was due to be opened by the comedian Jack Radcliffe but unfortunately he had to call off at the last minute. Our new Minister (whose packing cases still lay unopened on his new manse floor) saved the day. For the opening David stood up on a bench and to loud claps and cheers he began his opening remarks "You didn't give me much time..." but David didn't need much time to make a speech or deliver a sermon.

I vividly recall David telling me about changing his prepared sermon – he was walking from his vestry into the body of the kirk when he paused and looking around his congregation he decided that this was not the sermon for that day. By the time he got into the pulpit he had completely changed his sermon. This was indeed the brilliance of the man David Black.

The garden fete was a good beginning for David's long and fruitful ministry here at Mearnskirk. The afternoon allowed him to move about freely among his dear people – talking and listening, and getting to know his congregation. This allowed him to settle in quickly with us.

The manse was a very homely place and nobody was ever kept at the door but always invited in – not to the best room, but to the kitchen where the kettle was always on the boil. David's wife Betty would rustle up tea, coffee and scones or cakes. It was indeed a lovely way to relax and feel at home.

Jesus said "Come unto me all who are heavy laden and I will give you rest" Sitting around the kitchen table, David's opening remarks would go something like "Tell me what's troubling you?" "What's worrying you?". You will no doubt wonder why I say all this – suffice to say that on many occasions I was one of those thankful visitors.

It was with great sadness in my heart, and indeed the hearts of his dear people, that David announced in 1978 that he had been called to Cleish (later to be linked to Fossaway). David always began his pastoral letters with these words "My Dear People" – such tender, affectionate and loving words.

Sadly David's wife Betty passed away in December 1979. Five years later David was fortunate to meet Elizabeth Nicholson and they married on Christmas Day in 1983. They had two very happy years together until David's death on the 4th of January 1986.

David Arthur, born in 1926, is currently one of the longest serving Elders on the Session at Mearns Kirk. Ordained in 1974, he is still actively involved in all aspects of church life.

John O'Hara Thomson   1951-1959

John was born on 9th March 1908 at Annbank, Ayrshire, the son of Hugh Thomson and Christina O'Hara. He was educated at Annbank Primary School and Ayr Academy.

His further education was at Glasgow University where he received his MA in 1930 and Trinity College from where he received a bachelor of divinity with special distinction in the New Testament in 1933. He was licensed by the Presbytery of Ayr in 1933 and was assistant minister at Glasgow Camphill in 1933.

He was ordained and inducted to his first charge on 26 September 1933 at Clydebank Union Church, where he remained until transferred to Uddingston Trinity in 1940. He transferred and was inducted to Mearns on 12 September 1951. He died in office on 6 December 1959.

Alfred Drummond Duff MA   1929-1939 and 1943-1951

Alfred Drummond Duff was called to Mearns Parish Kirk in 1929 after the departure of his predecessor, The Rev. David Scott, to Canada. He was born at Kilmeny, Islay, on 26th January 1891 as the son of Alexander D. Duff, Minister of Oban.

He was educated at Oban and Glasgow High Schools and University of Glasgow. Licensed by the Presbytery of Lorne 26th December 1916; assistant at Maxwell Parish, Glasgow; Lieutenant in Argyll and Sutherland Highlanders in European War; ordained 14th November 1917. He was married on 25th October 1917 to Edith, daughter of Thomas Hart and Jane Thomson.

A man of his times; He saw active service in the Great War as a Lieutenant in the 11th Argyll and Sutherland Highlanders and he was seriously wounded losing his right arm.

At the outbreak of hostilities in 1939 he joined the 51st Highland Division and was senior chaplain. The 51st Highland Division was part of the British Expeditionary Force that went to France in May 1940 to support the French Army and keep them in the war. The 51st Division was attached to the French 9th Army Corps and was under French operational command.

In the aftermath of the Dunkirk evacuation, the unemployed German divisions there were sent to St Valery-en-Caux, where the 51st Division was billeted, west of the river Seine and attacked the French 9th Army Corps.

REPATRIATED CHAPLAIN

Among the repatriated prisoners of war welcomed at Leith by Lady Darling yesterday was the Rev. A. Drummond Duff, of Mearns Church, Newton Mearns. He was captured at St Valery in June, 1940, when senior chaplain to the 51st Division. He lost an arm in the last war, in which he fought as a combatant officer with the Argyll and Sutherland Highlanders.

Rev. Duff being welcomed home at Mearns Cross

Ministers of Mearns - Past and Present

The battle lasted from 5-13 June 1940, with the remnants of the 51st Highland Division being taken prisoner. He was repatriated in 1943. Rev. Duff was responsible for the replacement of the weathercock on the church spire. The story is that two farmers, who were making their way home quite merry from the Red Lion Inn, apparently decided to use the weathercock for target practice, shooting off its tail.

While Rev. Duff was a prisoner of war, he met Captain Holmes of Hazelden in a prisoner of war camp. Captain Holmes made a good Scot's promise to have the weathercock replaced should they both survive the war. Both duly did and in the late 1940's a new phosphor bronze weathercock was made and placed upon the steeple.

For readers who were taught or can remember the imperial system of weights and measures, it weighs two and a half hundredweights 2.5 cwts. For the modern reader the intellectual exercise for today is to calculate the weight in kilograms of the weathercock given a conversion factor of 1Kg = 2.2lbs

Rev. Duff died on 10 January 1951.

Mearns Kirk Boys Brigade around 1930. Rev. Drummond Duff, David Black and Tom Maver first Captain

David Scott MA   1915-1929

Born at Broughty Ferry in 1888 and educated at the High School of Dundee and St Andrew's University, he was Assistant Minister at the Barony Parish in 1913 and ordained on 21 April 1915.

Appointed minister at Mearns Parish Kirk from 1915 to 1929 when he voluntarily left the parish in May that year to take up a position at the Knox Crescent Presbyterian Church in Montreal. He saw active service as a soldier, having served in the Great War as a Chaplain to the 15th Scottish Division, seeing action in France and Flanders during 1917. David Scott initiated the campaign for the renovation of the church building and its extension, which was later finished by his successor.

He is shown here in centre foreground with his Kirk Session; the photograph is thought to be from 1927 just before he left for Canada.

David Scott returned later to Scotland and died at St Andrews in June 1945.

James Hutchison Cockburn MA DD   1908- 1915

He was born at Paisley in 1882 the son of a school master. He studied at Glasgow University receiving degrees in Divinity and Arts. In 1908 he was ordained in Mearns Kirk and served there until 1914 when he was transferred to Battlefield Church. Although he only served at Mearns Kirk for a brief time he had a very successful career. The photograph shown above and signed by him was on display in the Session House.

He served as a chaplain in the British Army during the Great War, seeing action in France, Egypt and East Africa.

On conclusion of hostilities he returned to Scotland and was appointed minister at Dunblane Cathedral where he served for several years. During the 1920's and 30's he served on the committee on the reunification of the churches. During the Second World War he was Moderator of the General Assembly of the Church of Scotland from 1941-42. He later became a chaplain to King George VI. He went on to an international church career in the 1950s with the World Council of Churches and was the author of several books on Church history.

James Cockburn died on 20 June 1973.

Ministers of Mearns - Past and Present

Mungo Reid MA. DD   1868-1908

Mungo Reid was Minister at Mearns Kirk from 1868 to 1908. He was born at Glasgow in 1838, the second son of Mungo Reid and Jessie Heron. He was educated at the High School and at Glasgow University where he was a distinguished scholar in the classics and Hebrew, receiving his MA in 1859. His personal bible, which is still in family hands, is a Hebrew text.

He was licensed by the Presbytery of Islay in 1863, and was assistant minister at St Andrew's Parish in Glasgow. In 1865 he was ordained to Lochgelly where he was minister until transfer to Mearns Kirk in July 1868. Rev. Reid was the longest serving minister at Mearns Kirk in modern times, having served his parish for forty years. His mother and son are buried in the church graveyard; He retired from his ministry at Mearns in 1908.

Mungo Reid with his wife Isabella Hamilton Pearson, a descendant of the Pearson family of Greenbank House, at the wedding of their daughter Ada to Charles Paterson in 1917.

Donald MacKellar   1834-1868

Born at Knapdale in Argyllshire and studied at the University of Glasgow. Donald was licensed by the Presbytery of Haddington on 12 December 1826 and presented by Sir Michael Shaw Stewart of Ardgowan (Bart) and ordained on 20 February 1834. He was clerk of the Presbytery from 1834-1868. He never married and died on 9th January 1868.

This is the only known surviving photograph of him and is the first photograph of any Mearns Kirk minister; the origins of it however are unknown. Rev. MacKellar wrote the account of the parish for the New Statistical Account of Scotland in 1834.

I have used some of the information supplied by him here. I have also tried to date the image from the clothing worn by Rev. MacKellar, but am unable to get any definitive references as to style etc., although the clothing looks to be from about the later 1850's. If this date can be relied on, then this is possibly one of the first 'wet plate' photographs taken using a system that was only invented in the 1850's.

Ministers of Mearns - Past and Present

George McLatchie MA DD   1788 - 1833

Was born at Glasgow on 5 April 1757; the son of schoolmaster Robert. M McLatchie. He studied at Glasgow University, receiving his MA in 1774. He was licensed by the Presbytery of Glasgow in 1778 and presented to the kirk by Sir Michael Stewart of Blackhall (Bart) on 7 February 1788. He was ordained assistant and successor on 11 April 1788 and died a bachelor on 13 August 1833. He was the tutor of John Wilson, author, who wrote under the pen name 'Christopher North' who resided with him at the manse for some time. He was responsible for the information regarding the origins of Newton Mearns village and the history of the district for Sinclair's Statistical Account of Scotland, now called the 'Old Statistical Account'.

Alexander Cruikshank   1752

Was born in Aberdeenshire in 1724 and was the son of a merchant. He studied at Marischal College Aberdeen and Glasgow University (MA 1742) He was licensed by the Presbytery of Haddington in 1748 and presented by Sir Michael Stewart of Blackhall (Bart) and ordained on 26 September 1752. He was one of the longest serving ministers at Mearns Parish Kirk, having been minister for thirty nine years and he had the duty of training his successor George McLatchie. He died on 22 January 1791.

George Macvey MA.   1733

Born at Glasgow on in 1688 he received his MA, from Glasgow University in 1707. He was chaplain to Mrs Stewart of Blackhall. Licensed by the Presbytery of Glasgow in 1717, he was ordained in 1733. He died in 1751 aged 63 years.

Henry Hunter   1713

He was born in 1681 the son of Patrick Hunter of Hunterston. He was educated at Glasgow University and presented to the kirk by John Stewart of Blackhall and ordained 28th April 1713. He died on 29th November 1731.

James MacDougall   1691

Was licensed by the Presbytery of Paisley on 21 January 1691 and ordained on 24 September 1691. He died in May 1712 and has been described as an honest, painful, gospel minister. He married in 1692 and had a daughter Susanna, who married the writer Alexander Stevenson from Irvine.

Ministers of Mearns - Past and Present

John Glen   1688

He was minister at Mearns from 1688 to 1691. He was educated at the University of Glasgow, having been bursar there in 1676. He was licensed by the Presbytery of Glasgow on 9 November 1687 and ordained on 27 February 1688. He was the first minister of Mearns Kirk after the revolution of 1688 and the abolition of episcopacy. He died sometime between 8 July 1691 and 15 September 1691; the exact date is unknown.

James Inglis   1686

The last of the Curates at Mearns Kirk, he was installed as minister on 22 May 1686 and deprived at the revolution in 1688. Nothing else is known about him other than he later became minister of Muthill in Perthshire.

John Taylor M.A.   1681

He was transferred to this parish from Libberton in Lanarkshire and presented to the Kirk by Sir Archibald Stewart of Blackhall (Bart) on 29 April 1681 and installed as minister sometime before 13 July 1681. He transferred to a second charge sometime before 10 November 1685.

Robert Fleming M.A. 1669

Transferred to the parish from Minnigaff in Dumfriesshire and was installed on 7 January 1669. He was the longest serving curate at Mearns Kirk and would have been party to much of the history of this area such as the Battles of Louden Hill and Bothwell Bridge in 1679. He was quoted earlier in chapter two regarding the conduct of the people here. He was transferred to Kirkintilloch sometime after the 4th May 1681.

James Taylor M.A.   1665

Prior to answering his call, James Taylor was a school master at Kilmarnock. He obtained his MA from Glasgow University in 1627 and was ordained to Greenock in 1640. He joined the Resolutioners in 1651. The Resolutioners were a faction within the church that supported the Kirk Resolutions of 14 December 1650 that would readmit royalist supporters of the King and the Engagers into the army to defend Scotland against an English invasion. He was transferred and admitted to Mearns Kirk on 20 July 1665. He died in March 1668.

Ministers of Mearns - Past and Present

William Thomson M.A.　　　1653
He received his M.A. from the University of Edinburgh on 30 July 1646 and was ordained on 11 August 1653. He was deprived by Act of Parliament on 11 June and Decreet of Privy Council on 1st October 1662. He is also mentioned in Chapter Two when the order of the Privy Council is enforced and he and his family are turned out of the manse by Government troops.

John Burnett　　　1652
Chaplain to Lord Wemyss, he was called to the parish in 1652 but probably did not accept.

David Gemmill M.A.　　　1650
He received his MA from Glasgow University in 1643. He was a minister of a Presbyterian congregation in Ireland the location of which is unspecified. However, it is known that he left there due to persecution. He was admitted here temporarily on 10 September 1650 and died in July 1651.

Hugh Cunningham M.A.　　　1649
Minister at Ray in Ireland, he was admitted here […] '… *until a door be opened for return to his own charge*' […] on 1st November 1649. He went to Erskine in 1651.

John Maxwell MA 1629(?) and 1645
Of Auldhouse: transferred from Eastwood to St Mungo's Glasgow sometime after 14th May 1629, having charge of the west quarter of the city. He departed the livings on 1st May 1639 for declining the jurisdiction of the General Assembly of 1638; sometime parson of Killyleagh in Ireland, he returned to Scotland in 1643 on account of the Irish Rebellion. He was minister of Eastwood again in 1645.

George Maxwell　　　1594
George Maxwell of Auldhouse was the son of John Maxwell of Auldhouse. He started his ministry at Neilston in 1592 and was transferred and admitted to Mearns Kirk in 1594. He was the non-resident minister mentioned at the end of chapter one and was ordered by the Presbytery of Paisley on 26 August 1635 to reside in his parish '… that he may visit the sick, and do the other incumbent duties…' He died in November 1648. George was married three times and had children with each wife, and according to records had twelve children overall.

Ministers of Mearns - Past and Present

Andrew Hay   1593

He was the son of the minister at Renfrew, also called Andrew Hay. He was minister at Erskine in 1590 and was transferred to Mearnskirk in 1593. On 7 May 1594 the Presbytery of Glasgow complained to the Presbytery of Paisley regarding his behaviour as mentioned in chapter one. From this evidence it appears that he was replaced by George Maxwell.

Biographical details become thin after this point in the records, and ministers with sole responsibility for the parish are few.

John Hay   1588
He was minister in 1588 and transferred to Renfrew in 1592

John Young	1586	Scripture Reader
Andrew Normand or Norman	1585	Scripture Reader

Patrick Adamson   1584
Minister of Paisley, Kilbarchan, Neilston and Mearns with charge at Mearns Kirk

Archibald Eglinton	1576-80	Scripture Reader
John Dobie	1575-6	Scripture Reader
Walter Stewart	1575	Scripture Reader

Ministers of Mearns - Past and Present

Pre Reformation times

There is very little known about some of those that had charge at Mearns Kirk during the Middle Ages. The following information comes from my copy of the Walker booklet shows in Appendix 1 additional information that has in some instances proved difficult to verify to my satisfaction.

1564 Thomas Dickson

1547 John Wilson

1490 Martin Reid

1432 John Rede

Nicholas De Otterburn aged 22 when he took responsibility for Mearns Kirk in 1418. He studied at St Andrew's University and was later Precentor of Glasgow. He relinquished his charge in 1432.

Before 1418 John De Hawyk, later Precentor of Glasgow and Papal Chaplain; resigned in 1418 in favour of Nicholas de Otterburn

Before 1409 John De Carruthers, of Dieger

1386 John Gardiner, of Brechin

John Gerland; Resigned in 1386 in favour of John Gardiner

Before 1386 but after 1380 Nicholas De Irwyn

1380 Findlay De K, of St Andrews

1300 Alan, Vicar

1190 Phillip, Priest

1163 Helia De Perthic
He is traditionally known as the first minister here, the founder of the Anglo Norman Church at Mearns, Prebend at and later Canon of Glasgow.

Ministers of Mearns - Past and Present

Kirk Session

The controlling body of the church is the Kirk Session. It is generally responsible in its modern form, through its various committees, for the upkeep of the church buildings and the paying of any accounts due.

In previous centuries the Kirk Session was the controlling court of the church parish, and as has been alluded to in previous chapters, they were responsible for the discipline of wayward parishioners and on occasion ministers!

There have been occasions in the past where due to the reluctance of people to serve on the Kirk Session that it has died out altogether. This happened here in 1855, and a petition was raised at the Presbytery of Paisley for the imposition of a Kirk Session at Mearns with the specific duty of receiving the retiring collection monies.

There are a few photographs of ministers with their Kirk Sessions available and I have included them here, with the exception of David Scott, who is shown earlier in this chapter. The photographs that follow provide an interesting social and historical snapshot of life in the Parish.

The earliest known Mearns Kirk Session photograph - circa 1904

Mungo Reid and his Kirk Session thought to be from the early part of the Twentieth Century. Given the formal attire of the subjects, this could be just before Mungo Reid retires. This was taken at the entrance to the old manse.

Ministers of Mearns - Past and Present

This is taken after 1932 with the new session house in the background. Rev. Drummond Duff is seated centre foreground.

A jump now of over 40 years and the 1978 Kirk session which contained women as elders for the first time. Seated in foregound is Rev. David Black.

Ministers of Mearns - Past and Present

Taken in 1994 with the Minister, Rev. Roderick Campbell seated in the foreground. Note the increase in the number of women as elders.

Kirk Session photograph taken in June 2012.

PART TWO

Mearns Kirk – The People Past and Present

The People - Past and Present

Introduction

This book started out as a project for the 200th anniversary in 2013. The intention was to simply update the booklet Mr Walker had published thirty years earlier. Initially the current photos were to feature in the commemorative programme booklet for 2013, but since the Walker booklet showed photos of groups and organisations, it felt only right to follow the history part of this book with a chapter on the people of the Mearns Kirk family, capturing this moment in time for the next generation.

The names of everyone appearing on the following pages, especially the group photographs, are listed in Appendix C.

Marianne MacGregor
April 2013

The Kirk Session 2012 with current and retired elders.

The People - Past and Present

Marje Gillies
Session Clerk

Role of Session Clerk

My role as (the first female) Session Clerk at Mearns Kirk started in 2008 when I took over from John Mercer who was immensely experienced, having spent two long spells as Session Clerk. I am grateful to John for his efficient handover and his support, when needed since then.

I've learned the role by doing what's needed and the basics have become second nature; for example, setting the agendas with the Minister for Kirk Session meetings, taking minutes for Kirk Session and Conveners' meetings, organising the annual Elders' Coffee Morning along with many of the Elders, welcoming new church members and working alongside our secretary. The role also includes having oversight of the work of all church groups - I see the minutes but don't attend all meetings!

The People - Past and Present

There are always other, sometimes one-off things to attend to e.g. selection and recruitment of some staff, overseeing the introduction of new employment contracts following changes by the General Trustees (until Finance took this over), co-ordinating responses to consultations such Same Sex Relationships and the Ministry, jointly supporting the Parish Grouping meetings taking turns with the other four Session Clerks in our Parish Grouping and being involved in meetings for the Presbytery Plan.

In the past year, Eleanor Boyd, who became Assistant Session Clerk in 2011, and I oversaw the changes in the way we serve Communion. Eleanor has responsibility for the Districts and for Health & Safety in addition to her other roles as an Elder and I am delighted that she agreed to take this new role on.

My role is a co-ordinating one – something which I enjoyed at work – and being able to do this for church is very important to me. I like a challenge and at times have not been disappointed! However, the special part of the role of Session Clerk is the people I've got to know and the firm friendships I've made with a number of people.

Eleanor Boyd
Assistant Session Clerk

Finally, I would like to thank our minister, Joe Kavanagh, for all his support, patience and understanding over the last five years. Perhaps the fact that when he asked if I would consider becoming Session Clerk I agreed to a one year trial and, almost five years later, I am still thoroughly enjoying my time as part of the life of Mearns Kirk.

M Gillies - 3 Sept 2012

The People - Past and Present

Marion McDonald
Church Officer

Marion took on this role in 1998 when the previous church beadle, Bert Dinsmor, retired after many years. In addition to her many tasks as a church officer, Marion is a Church Elder and as the Convenor of the Worship and Education Group often conducts services when the Minister is absent.

Anne Campbell
Assistant Church Officer

Andrea Gibson
Secretary

My work as the Church Secretary keeps me very busy throughout the year. It's great to be working in such a lively environment with all the various groups coming and going.

Marie Foulkes
Hallkeeper

I work as the hall keeper for the church halls. This brings me in to contact with lots of different groups and organisations and I enjoy getting to know all the different people involved.

The Fabric Committee

The Fabric Committee is responsible for the maintenance, upkeep and improvement of the various church properties - the kirk, the halls, the manse, the old session house, the car park and the glebe. It works to a budget that is set each year, covering expenditure on routine maintenance together with exceptional items.

In recent times, a significant amount of money has been spent repairing and replacing the flat roofs at the halls and the kirk with modern materials.

The Committee is responsible for organising and supervising the various projects including upgrading the sound and vision systems in the church and halls to mark our Bicentenary celebrations in 2013.

The Finance Committee

The Finance Committee is responsible for raising and safeguarding the finances of the Church. It ensures that all expenditure is incurred prudently and in line with the annual budget. The Finance Committee looks after the weekly givings and all other funds raised and donated – with Gift Aid being a vital part. Other matters covered include salaries, leases, insurances and the preparation of annual accounts. To ensure that the Church has sufficient income to meet all its continuing costs, every few years a Stewardship Campaign is organised, the next campaign arising will be in 2014.

The Safeguarding Committee

Safeguarding is about protecting children and vulnerable adults in, or known to, Church congregations. We recognise that we have a duty to ensure a safe Church for all and have a zero tolerance approach to harm or abuse of people; any type or level is unacceptable.

Mearns Kirk has a Safeguarding Coordinator; we have a safe recruitment and selection procedure for staff and volunteers working with children and "protected" adults, which includes all workers getting checked under the PVG regulations (Protection of Vulnerable Groups) and attending training relevant to meet the learning needs of different groups of people in the Church.

Isobel Dawson – Co-ordinator shown here on the right with Stewart Drummond and Margaret Hamilton.

The Pastoral Group

A group of church members who visit and befriend the housebound and elderly.

The People - Past and Present

Music in our Church

Choir with Organist, Doris Watson (far left) on 25th March 2012

Before 1932, Mearns Kirk was a square building with the pulpit located on the south wall and a raised platform in front of the pulpit accommodating the communion table, chair and the choir. Music has always been at the heart of worship - a small organ was situated west of the pulpit, beside the vestry door. The bellows for the organ were pumped by a lad who frequently fell asleep during the sermon and had to be wakened by the beadle to power the organ for the last hymn! Before worship, the choir used to assemble in the Old Session House and then they would process up to the church for the service.

There have been various organists over the years, of course - Jean Binning, Joe Oakley, Sandy McPherson, Malcolm Sim (currently organist at Glasgow Cathedral), Jean Binning (for a second time) and now, Doris Watson. The earliest recorded photo of the choir was taken in the 1930s and there is a photo of an outing to Killiecrankie on Coronation Day, 1937. More recent outings have been to Largs, Crutherlands, Whitecraigs, Cathcart Castle and, this year, Williamwood Golf Clubs where we have enjoyed annual dinners.

The People - Past and Present

The Choir has performed 'Night of Miracles' in our Church, Newton Mearns Parish Church and Cathcart South. Each year we sing at the Woman's Guild Christmas meeting, enjoying mince pies and mulled wine after our performance.

Sunday by Sunday, the Church Choir leads the congregation in our praises to God. At the moment, we are an enthusiastic group of six men and fourteen women performing old and new anthems to enhance the worship. Our music is varied and we have had several beautiful anthems sent from Australia, written by Howard Davies.

After visiting our church one summer, he wrote an anthem specially for us and named the tune 'Mearnskirk'. We have lots of fun and fellowship as we learn these anthems and hymns under the direction of our organist, so, if you can sing, we would be delighted to see you in the new hall on Thursday evenings.

Written by Doris Watson, Organist, Summer 2012

The choir and friends - Performance of Stainer's Crucifixion on Palm Sunday, 24th March 2013 – a very successful evening as part of the 2013 Bi-centenary Celebrations

The People - Past and Present

A visit in 2009 from Howard Davies and his wife Sheina, who are Salvation Army Officers and live in Australia.

Howard writes both choral and band music which is played and sung throughout the world. The Choir had the privilege to perform Howard's most recent song 'I won't forget the hands of Christ' for Easter in 2013.

Choir with organist Sandy MacPherson and Rev. Roderick Campbell - possibly taken at Easter 1988 given the Easter hymns on the board.

Choir – possibly at Easter 1984

Choir in 2008 with retiring organist Jean Binning

The People - Past and Present

The Woman's Guild

Our Guild was formed just over 100 years ago, in March, 1911. Then, as now, meetings were held on a regular basis and consisted of an opening hymn, Bible reading and prayer. The evening's speaker was then introduced, after which there were questions and a vote of thanks. Tea was served and Guild business was discussed. The evening concluded with a closing hymn and prayer.

We continue to follow this formula, but looking back over the 65 years of syllabi we hold in records, perhaps a talk on "Temperance" (Nov 1954) might not prompt much enthusiasm today. Thirteen years on "Know your joints" might have proved disappointing for those looking to find out more about drugs! Generally though, we have continued to enjoy varied programmes throughout each session of talks, entertainment, outings and theatre visits.

We have always benefited from a wealth of talent from the ranks of our own membership (Guild Players and Guild Singers). I'm sure many will recognise these ladies though some twenty years have passed!

In the early days, meetings were held weekly. On alternate weeks, a Working Party was held. Here, groups of ladies either stitched sewed or even crocheted. Much lively banter ensued in these busy sessions. The items produced were stored away and later sold at our sale of work. Money from this would be saved and used towards our Church. The Work Party was disbanded many years ago.

The Mearns Kirk Woman's Guild – at the AGM on 4th April 2012

The People - Past and Present

In late February 1913, almost two years after the Guild was formed, a presentation was made to the Church of an oak Communion table and large chair. These items were in position in time for the Dedication Service on 1st March. Dedication was by Rev. A M Maclean, BD, Paisley Abbey, assisted by Rev. J D Brown MA Whiting Bay and the minister of the Parish. At this time the Guild also supplied a flower vase.

The Guild over the century has continued the original theme of presenting gifts to the Church. Other early gifts include a linen chest, Communion linen and silverware. The blue carpet and clothes for use at communion were also contributions from the Guild. For the 2013 celebrations Jessie Campbell has renewed the blue velvet collection bags with the contribution from the Guild .

Much of the tradition of the early days of the guild has not changed. We still remain committed to serving our church, to supporting charities and groups and to providing an environment of fellowship, friendship and support.

The Woman's Guild Singers (1985-95) gave many performances in the area - here at Seamill Hydro for the Rotary Club – May 1989

The last performance at Joe's induction 1998

The People - Past and Present

The Woman's Guild Players

Our Guild continues to meet every two weeks from September to April. Meetings still take the same form as 1911 with talks, demonstrations, musical and other social evenings filling our syllabus. We present our speakers with a cheque towards their particular charity and we continue too, to support charities including Erskine Hospital, Age Concern Eastwoodhill and the Lodging House Mission.

In 2011, we celebrated our centenary culminating with a very successful Centenary Dinner held in our church hall on March 23rd. Our own members provided an entertaining evening sourced from bygone days. We still continue to benefit from talented friends to entertain us. For example, the vision of "Three White Brides" still remains - don't ask! As we look forward to our second century, our photograph clearly shows the friendship and fellowship that we continue to enjoy together as Mearns Kirk Woman's Guild.

The Woman's Guild celebrating 100 years – 1911-2011

It is clear that our guild is very much alive. We look forward to taking part in the special celebrations of 2013. If there are any ladies who are not members, we would extend a warm hand of friendship to you and encourage you to come along!

Written by Jessie Campbell, Summer 2012

The Mission Group

The Mission Group in 2012 was under the leadership of Tom Greig and covered a very wide range of areas, responding to challenges that arise not only in our local community, but also nationally and internationally.

Their work supports the Lodging House Mission for the Homeless in Glasgow, CrossReach and their local care homes, Eastwoodhill and Williamwood House. Members of the Mission group take part in the Chaplaincy at Victoria Hospital and also join the Mearnskirk Hospital Singers.

Other initiatives are the 'Spare Seat Club' offering transport to non-drivers, making new friends via the Friendship Book at church, the used Stamp Appeal, Fairtrade initiatives including a Fairtrade Lunch and delivering Easter and Christmas cards around the entire Parish.

The Mission group was instrumental in our church being awarded the Green Flag as an Eco Congregation, an ongoing effort to recycle and re-use to conserve our natural resources.

The People - Past and Present

Friendship Singers

A group of ladies, led by Jean Binning, who offer a varied entertainment programme to groups. We sing, give readings, and offer opportunities for reminiscence to, for example, church groups and care home residents.

Our theme song is

> Come and discover the love that is found,
> In meeting and greeting friends all around,
> The clasp of a handshake, the smile on a face,
> Reflecting God's love and His wonderful grace.
>
> When we come in friendship to worship The Lord,
> We come in the spirit of loving accord
> Through faith that grows stronger we find peace of mind
> Encouraged by friends that are loving and kind.

Mearns Kirk Friendship Club

Back in 1990 the then minister of Mearns Kirk saw a need in the community for the bringing together of the elderly residents who were lonely or unable to get out and about on their own. To this end an enterprising young lady of the session offered, with the help of friends, to run a club once a fortnight, providing afternoon tea, interesting talks and entertainment.

Very quickly offers of entertainment, home baking, transport and escorting to and fro came from all corners of the church and as word spread the numbers increased rapidly from 16 members to a roll of around 100.

Sadly none of the original helpers are involved today but the club is ably carried on by those who followed in their footsteps and some of the present helpers have given their dedicated service for almost 20 years.

Margaret Courts (Former Leader 2009-2013)

The Friendship Club

The People - Past and Present

The Friendship Club continues to thrive due to a wonderful group of helpers, bus drivers and car drivers who give so generously of their time and talents.

We meet on alternate Tuesdays from 1.45-3.15 p.m. in the Main Hall and welcome people from our own church, other churches, care homes and the wider community – people of faith, people of none.

Members enjoy a varied programme of musical entertainment, afternoon tea and chat. Our annual outing is in May. Come and join us.

The Flower Committee

We at Mearns Kirk are very lucky that so many members contribute money each Sunday to the Flower Fund. This ensures the church always has a beautiful display thanks to our willing flower arrangers.

We are also fortunate to have volunteers who take the flowers each Sunday to the sick and bereaved in the parish.

At Harvest Thanksgiving we decorate the church and distribute around forty arrangements to church members chosen by our Minister Joe. We also enjoy decorating the church at Christmas.

Rosemary Baillie – Flower Convenor

Youth Club Planting Mission (2005-2007)

In 2005 Mearns Kirk's youth ministry team invited the Impact Mission to help set up youth work for the large group of young people who had outgrown the Sunday School.

Once a month the Impact team would arrive on a Saturday afternoon to prepare and set up the youth club for the evening, helped by Mearns Kirk volunteers. The team would stay in the halls overnight and attend the Sunday services in the morning. The MPK Club proved to be very popular and no effort was spared to organise a full evening of activities and events.

In June 2007, with the MPK Club now fully established and running fortnightly, the Impact team moved on to their next project, handing over to the Mearns Kirk team who by then had employed a part-time youth worker. Several youth workers later, Emma Stevenson took on the job in February 2010 and stepped down only recently in March 2013.

To commemorate the occasion, on 2 June 2007, a young oak tree, donated by Liz Gourlay, was planted at the border of the wildlife garden.

Sunday Club with Moderator

The children with their parents and leaders of the Sunday Club on the 19th February 2013 with the Right Rev. Albert Bogle, Moderator of the Church of Scotland, and Rev. Joe Kavanagh in between the children in the front row. Notice the oak tree (with brown leaves) in the centre behind the group which was planted in 2007.

The People - Past and Present

Sunday Club Staff

The aim of the Sunday Club is help children discover God and Faith for themselves. The Leaders work very hard to make it a joyful and creative experience and the wider church family really do try and make church a good place to come to. In this day and age when there are so many influences upon us all, you have the opportunity to sow good seed in your children's hearts by giving them the chance to share in the life of God's family.

Mearns Kirk is very fortunate to have a very lively Sunday Club, but like many other churches, we are in constant need for more teachers on a Sunday morning.

1st Mearns Guides

1st Mearns Guides was established in December 1923. Guides is for girls aged 10 years old and up. 1st Mearns guides meet for two hours every Thursday evening where we do various activities to help extend the guides knowledge and skills. The girls can also gain various interest badges and also Challenge badges that recognise their participation in guiding over a period of time. These badges build towards the Baden Powell Challenge Award which is the highest award a Guide can achieve.

Mother and Toddler Group

The group has existed for many years meeting in the halls every Wednesday at 9:45am until 11:30am.

The People - Past and Present

The Keep Fit Group

The Keep Fit Class was started by Nicki Edgar, the local police woman, when the newly built church halls were opened in 1970. I joined the class and after only two weeks Nicki, who lived in the (former) police house on Capelrig Road adjacent to the Marks & Spencer car park, asked if I would take over as she was pregnant. I have taken the class ever since then – celebrating 40 years in 2010.

In the early years we had a lot of young Mums, so there was a crèche which was run by a rota system organised by the Mums. Some of the Mums are still in the class to this day! Over the years the Keep Fit Group has donated money to various charities and disaster areas. Our main charity we have given to for 32 years is East Park in Maryhill, who were founded in 1874 to educate and support children with physical and learning disabilities. We have also contributed to the gardens around our church: we planted azaleas' and rhododendrons in the Millennium Garden in June 2000 (which is now the Memorial Garden) and two oak trees, one in the wildlife garden and another one at the back of the church near Mearns Road at a total cost of £560 half of which was paid for by East Renfrewshire Council. In 2012 we joined the Badminton Group and organised a Bridge Drive raising £913 for the Bi-centenary funds.

Over the past 42 years many long lasting friendships were formed while keeping fit – and to this day we welcome new members not just from our church but from our community around us. We meet every Thursday morning at 10am in the halls.

May MacIntosh –Keep Fit Leader

The People - Past and Present

Keep Fit Group in 2000

May MacIntosh with Rev. Joe Kavanagh in 2010 celebrating May's 40th anniversary as the Keep Fit leader.

Ladies Walking Club

The Ladies Walking Group was formed in March 2009. It aims to provide a safe walking environment for the ladies of Mearns Kirk. More importantly, the group enables ladies to make new friendships and have fun as well as to share knowledge of local places, history, architecture, nature etc., with each other and with Church Magazine readers.

The group meets monthly on a Wednesday at 1.30 pm, in the church car park. Car sharing is available but a moderate level of fitness is required. The walks last approximately 2 hours - with a coffee stop!

Plans for the future include increasing the number of regular walkers and maintaining the good health of the current members. Less rain would be good!

The People - Past and Present

Mixed Badminton Club

The Club was resurrected in 2011 after several years of inactivity as some of us felt we would be better trying to run around and stretch for the odd shuttle than sit in our armchairs every evening throughout the winter. We have 12 members so far and meet every second Wednesday evening at 7.30pm, alternating the use of the main hall with The Guild. We enjoy the fun of the game and all the chatting/ meeting/ laughing with friends and making new friends. We couldn't have too big a group because of having only one court - but maybe a couple of extras could be encouraged to come along and join us - nobody is too good at the game!

For the 2013 Celebrations our little group organised a 6 mile hike interspersed with local history talks followed by a BBQ and folk night which managed to raise over £1.200 for our efforts. We all worked hard and had great fun on the night, with lots of support from family, friends and neighbours as well as the Church family. It was great to walk with others who love their local countryside, to get to know more about the history of our area and to meet new people. Next summer we plan another walk / barbeque.

The People - Past and Present

Our Photographer - John Hamilton

Many of the photos you find in this book, inside and outside the church building, were taken by John Hamilton. To create a snapshot of life at Mearns Kirk, John, who is pictured here, visited all the church groups and organisations during 2012 - often more than once - to take photographs of the people without whom we would not be a church family.

John passed away unexpectedly on the 2nd January 2013 without seeing the completed works. We are very grateful to Margaret, his wife, for allowing us to remember John in this way.

The team responsible for the 2013 bi-centenary celebrations started preparations three years earlier.

The three members of the 2013 Team pictured here from left to right with Rev. Joe Kavanagh are Mandy Stewart, Marianne MacGregor and David Bremner.

Appendices - Bibliography

Mearns Kirk prior to 1932.

Appendices

Bibliography

Appendix A

Latin Translations

Latin extract from Register of Paisley Abbey on Donation of Helia de Perthyk circa 1179

Heilas clericus filius Fulberti omnibus sancte matris ecclesie filiis et fidelibus salutem. Sciatis me dedisse et hac mea carta confirmasse ecclesie Sancti Jacobi et Sancti Mirini et Sancte Milburge de Passlet et monachis ibidem Deo serventibus, ecclessiam de Merness, cum omnibus pertinentiis suis, in terris et aquis, in planis et pascuis, libere et quiete, imperpetuam elemosinam, pro anima Walteri, filii Alani et pro anima Herberti glassguensis episcopi, et pro animabus patris et matris mee, et benefactorum meorum, et pro animabus antecessorum meorum et successorum,et pro salute mea et Alani advocati nostri et fratrum meorum.

Heilas the cleric, son of Fulbert, gives greetings to all the sons of Mother Church and to the faithful. Know ye, that I have given, by this my charter and confirmed to the church of St James and St Mirren, and to the monks of the Paisley Monastery in service of the Holy God there, the church of Merness, with all its appurtenances, in the earth and the waters, and in the planes of the pasture, freely and quietly, alms for ever , for the soul of Walter, son of Alan, and for the soul of the bishop Herbert of Glasgow, and for the souls of my father and mother, and benefactors, and of and for the souls of my ancestors and successors, and to thank Alan, patron to me and my brother.

Wilelmus Dei gratia rex Scotorum omnibus probis hominibus totius terre sue clerics et laicis salutem.

Sciant presentes et futuri me conssisse et hac carta mea confirmasse Deo et Ecclesie Sancti Mirini de Passlet et monachis ibidem Deo servientibus, donationem illam quam Helias de Pertheic eis fecit per consessionem Petri de Polloc fratris sui, de ecclesia de Merness:

Tenenda in liberam et perpetuam elemosinam ita libere, quiete, plenarie et honorifice sicut alias ecclesias suis liberius, quietus, plenius, et honorificentius tenent, et sicut carta predicti Helye testatur. Testibus hiis, Alano abbate Dunfermelyn, Hugone cancellario meo, Rollando filio Ucdred, comite Patricio, Wilelmo de Lyndsay, Phillipo de Walons, Roberto de Londe, Henrico de Cormannoc, apud Lanryk.

William, by the grace of God king of Scots, Greetings to all good men of the clergy and laity of the country.
I now present and future confer and by this my charter, confirm to God and the Holy Church of St Mirren at Paisley and monks there serving God; the church of Merness, donated to them by Elijah of Pertheic made with concession from Peter of Polloc his brother:
To hold in free and perpetual alms as freely, quietly, fully and honorably as the church to his other more freely, quietly, fully, and honorably hold, and Elias, as the charter of the aforesaid testifies. Witness the following, Alan, Abbot of Dunfermline, my chancellor Hugh, Rolland son Ucdred, Earl Patrick, William Lyndsay, Phillip of Wales, Robert of London, Henry of Cormannoc, with Lanryk.

First appearance of Alan as perpetual vicar of Mearns in deeds of Herbert Maxwell's land.
Circa 1177-99

Hiis testibus domino Ada rectore ecclesie de Liberton, domino Alano perpetuo vicario de Merness, Johanne de Maxwell domino de Polloc inferiori, domino Alano glassfurd milite, Waltero filio Gilberti, Johnanne clerico, Gilberto de Malotshok, et matheo de Flandre, et aliis. In cujus rei testimonium presentibus sigillum meum, una cum sigillo officialitatis curie Glasguensis, est appensum.

Witness; Master Ada the rector of the church of Liberton, Master Alan, the perpetual vicar of Merness, John Maxwell of the lower of the Polloc, Master Alan Glassford, Knight, Walter son of Gilbert, Johnanne clerk, Gilbert of Malotshok, and Matthew of Flanders, and others. In witness whereof my seal to the present, together with the Official seal of the court of Glasgow, is affixed to.

Appendix B

A discussion on the origins and age of the stone slab at Mearns Kirk

When updating the history of Mearns Kirk, I was pleasantly surprised to find a reference to a stone slab on the website that purported to be of Templar origin that was found during the 1931-2 renovations. It was found where the current Vestry stands, indeed, Rev. A Boyd -Scott, Minister at Newton Mearns Parish church mentions it in his book 'Old Days and Ways in Newton Mearns' and even he suggests that the argument for its origins to be a 'Templar grave marker' may be premature, But no one from the church comments on it at all, at least not that I could find, nor records where in relation to the East door it was found.

It appears that the origins of the idea that the stone is a Templar Grave marker comes from an examination of it by, Ludovic Mann, President of the Glasgow Archaeological Society 1931-34, and as it appears as possibly a 'Templar' stone in Boyd-Scott's book in 1938, then he must have seen it during this time, but left no written records that I can find.

Mann himself was a controversial character in Modern Scottish Archaeology; he was an insurance broker by trade, and a self-taught amateur archaeologist, conducting many excavations in the west of Scotland. His theories were for the time, outlandish, and some of his major theories were never published, but he did conduct some notable excavations.

The stone itself is quite remarkable, having only viewed the church website image of it, I was surprised just how misleading an impression that photograph gives. The stone itself is much larger than I first thought. It is 690mm wide, at least 200mm thick and about 1650mm tall and must weigh in easily at about half a ton, no surprise then for leaving it propped up against the east wall near to where it was found! It has relatively square edges and faces, meaning that it has been worked into this shape; it tapers slightly from top to bottom on the right side. The top surface appears to have been rounded off at the edges at some point during manufacture, giving the stone a bevelled surface; there are no other decorated faces or edges other than the top surface. The stone has a large Latin cross incised into its surface which runs the full length of the slab and is at a very slight angle, just off the centre line leaning to the right as shown above outlined in red.

Appendices - Bibliography

The top third of the stone shows the top part of the Latin cross in relief, i.e. proud of the surrounding surface, that starts in about 50mm from the top edge and the left hand side edge which may give rise to the slightly off centre aspect of the Latin Cross although this slant may be deliberate. It also seems that a portion of the stone has been lost from the top of it at the right hand end of the cross arm, resulting in a slightly shorter right hand cross arm than the left hand side.

An incised straight sword is shown on the right side slightly below the right arm of the cross, and disappears below the soil line. The sword image would appear to be the easiest dated given the information available on the internet and in the Kelvingrove Museum displays. I have used the Oakeshott system of sword classification as it appears to be the most common.

The type of sword appears to conform to the Oakeshott Xa2 description and is dated from 1050-1100AD. See the following reference http://www.myarmoury.com/feature_spotx.html which is where I have sourced some of the evidence to support the theory that this slab is from the 10th century.

Given the size of the slab, I am surprised that it was not found during the original remodelling of the church building. This leads me to believe that the slab became buried over time due to its weight and lost from memory, furthermore- that the remodelling of the church in 1813 did not extend into the eastern end of the church graveyard; as to the style and execution of the stone slab that required further research.

Appendices - Bibliography

I was grateful to Mr David Arthur for a collection of articles on ancient Christian monuments in the district, most notably the Capelrig Cross, which is in the collection of the Kelvingrove Art galleries and Museums. Included in this collection were some articles from *'The Society of Antiquaries of Scotland'* which related several articles on incised stone grave slabs in the West Dunbartonshire area. These articles were from the late 1920's and were concerned with the ruins of early Christian churches and graveyards that preceded the arrival of the Normans in the Twelfth Century. Although no definitive date could be gleaned from the slabs the common thread was that they were all found in churches that had a connection to an early Christian saint, such as St. Blane, St. Bride and St. Marnoch, all of whom were active in the west of Scotland from the 5th Century AD onwards.

The common theme here is that all the stones have an image of a sword on them. The cross styles are too varied to try and search for let alone estimate a date for. The cross guard on the Luss sword according to Oakeshott dates from about 950AD and the one from Kilmaronock is contemporary with Mearns that is from 1000-1150.

The overall length of the sword from pommel tip to where it enters the ground is 980mm. The height of the handle from the top of the cross guard to the pommel is 160mm. The width of the cross guard itself is 200mm; there are no other discernible markings on the sword. The Oakeshott sword style reference mentioned earlier takes the view that the handle and cross-guard are an important part of sword design for dating purposes. I said earlier that this stone tapers slightly from top to bottom on the right (sword) side, when researching this I came across information on Pictish standing stones, those that were markers, the most obvious examples of which are Crosses. I had considered that this might be an early church precincts marker, but the carvings would normally stop before the bottom of the stone to allow it to be set into the ground and leave the full markings visible, you would expect it also to be decorated with the same or a similar image on both sides none of these happen here; therefore I would suggest that this is a grave marker.

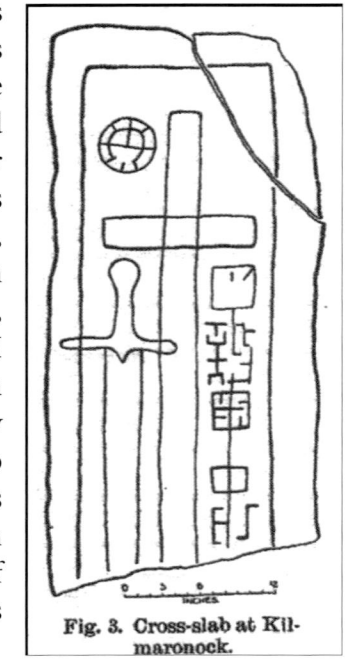

Fig. 3. Cross-slab at Kilmaronock.

Appendices - Bibliography

I relation to the sword image, I think that the sword depiction is of a commonly used weapon from that time; the Oakeshott style guide gives an origin for this type of sword in the Viking period in the west of Scotland from about 8th century onwards, their sword being a derivation of the Roman short sword. Therefore I think that the sculptor copied the design from an existing weapon onto the stone, the design of it being a derivation of the Viking sword, where the differences are at the disk shaped pommel at the end of the handle.

Standing crosses and incised slabs have been used to mark the precincts of holy places, standing crosses such as the Capelrig Cross is a clear example. The Latin cross incised on the slab is leaning slightly to the right as you look at it; there is a belief that this stylisation, either right leaning or left leaning from the vertical, has its foundation in the crucifixion story and the two other men that were crucified on the same day as Christ.

In refuting the contention that this slab is Templar in origin I would offer the previous stone slabs as evidence of a Christian culture in the west of Scotland that commemorated the passing of significant people who were recognised by symbols that represented their main occupation or reason for their demise.

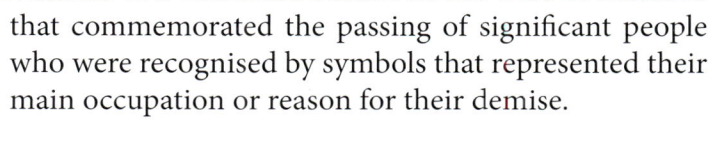

I would like to think that people who died in this area before the arrival of the Knights Templar were commemorated by their families in this manner. I would suggest that this is exactly what we have here, a grave marker for a fallen soldier and given the sword image, a man who was not part of a religious order, but in any event a Christian warrior from the time before the Templars.

We will never know for sure, however I would suggest that given the number of stones of a similar description and style found in other churches throughout west central Scotland it would support the conclusion that this stone is in the same style and dates from the 11th century.

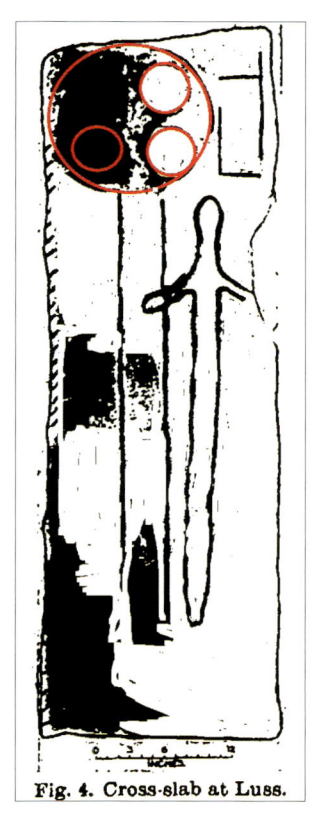

Fig. 4. Cross-slab at Luss.

Images from the *Society of Antiquaries* book dated 10 January 1927.

143

Appendix C

This appendix lists all the names of everyone shown in the photographs in this book to the best of our knowledge at the time.

Kirk Session with Mungo Reid (page 108)
Not all of the names are known, but the Congregational Directory and Statements of Accounts published in 1921-22 lists following Elders (with the date they were ordained in brackets):
John S. Downie (25.6.1893), James Barr (25.6.1893), John Glassford (23.6.1907), William Maver (23.6.1907), John Barr (23.6.1907), John B. Craig (26.10.1913), Robert Johnston (25.10.1913), James Bowman (8.2.1914)

Kirk Session with Drummond Duff (page 109)
From left to right (as taken from W.A.Walker):
Front row: JAS. McGhie, E. Johnstone, Rev. A.D. Duff, Henry Watson, JAS. Bowman, J.A. Barr
Back row: H.A. Frew, D. Scott, D. Black, William Maver, Robert Orr, J.D. Timothy, Robert Stewart, M. Cowan

Kirk Session with Rev. David Black – Photo taken in 1978 (page 109)
Left to right: Front row (seated):
Catherine Runciman, Duncan Campbell, Jean Peachey, Arthur McKirdy, May McIntosh (McColl at the time), Peter McCree, Matt Gillies, Rev. David Black, John Mercer, John Cunningham, Margaret Courts, Tom Adamson, Andrew Fairie, Ian Hutchison, Bill Russell

Second row: Gordon Wilson, Alistair Cameron, Douglas King, Jack Mowat, David Miller, David Kidd, Joe Britton, Jack Taylor, Gordon Calderwood, Alistair Hamilton, Dale Macfadyen, John Lawson, Mr Hyslop, George Kenneth Clark, Robert White, David Arthur, Jack Adye, Alex Fitzpatrick

Third row: James Hamilton, Tom Wilson, Donald Fraser, John Hudson, Ferrie Young, Terry McMurtrie, Jim Keating, George Cockburn, Charlie Williamson, Andrew Walker, Brian Harris, Alex Laird, Dennis Clark, Ray Malcolm, Bill Shaw, Bert Dinsmor

Appendices - Bibliography

Kirk Session with Rev. R. Campbell – Photo taken in 1994 (page 109)
From left to right: Front row (seated):
Catherine Runciman, Jack Taylor, Margaret Courts, John Mercer, John Skinner, Jack McDougall (Session Clerk), Rev. Roderick Campbell, Margaret Wilson, Norman Anderson, Jean Peachey, Dale Macfadyen, Robert White, David Kidd

Second row: David Miller, Bert Dinsmor, Alex West, May McIntosh, Jack Mowat, Isabelle Dyer, Martin Stirling, Margaret McColl, Joe Britton, Anne Scott, Hugh Brodie, Mary Deas, David Arthur, Alison Howarth, James Keating, Fiona Lyon, Ronnie Sinclair, Elizabeth Martin, Brian Jackson

Third row: Tom Hendry, Gordon Wilson, Frank McCarroll, Bill McDougall, Alistair Cameron, Ian Hutchison, James Goold (Lord), John Henderson, Douglas Graham, Bill Jenkins, Bob Weir, Alister McCormick, Alistair Hamilton

Kirk Session June 2012 (page 110)
Front row:
David Bremner, Marion MacDonald (Church Officer), Eleanor Boyd (Assistant Session Clerk), Marje Gillies (Session Clerk), Rev. Joe Kavanagh, Robert Paton (Treasurer), Ian Stubbs (Finance Convenor), Jimmy Brown, John Henderson (Fabric Convenor), Norman Anderson

Second row:
Donald Fraser, Stewart Drummond, Marshall Wyllie, Liz Gourlay, Bill Jenkins, Marianne MacGregor

Third row:
Isobel Dawson, Ann Campbell, Sandra McFarlane, Violet Kimble, Ronnie Sinclair, Kay Galloway, Liz Ronald, Mary Deas, Heather Anderson

Fourth row (on stage):
Sandy Watson, Irene McKerral, Jim McKerral, Anne Scott, Stewart Cairns, Isabelle Dyer, Gordon Wilson, Heather Gilchrist, Lindsay McKendrick

Appendices - Bibliography

Kirk Session with current and retired Elders in 2012 (page 112)
Left to right:
Front row: Anne Scott, Mary Deas, Sandra McFarlane, Marion MacDonald (Church Officer), Marje Gillies (Session Clerk), Rev. Joe Kavanagh, Eleanor Boyd (Assistant Session Clerk), Liz Ronald, Isabelle Dyer, Irene McKerral

Second row: Ian Hutchison (retired– former Fabric Convenor), Dr. David Kidd (retired), Jack McDougall (retired- former Session Clerk), Jack Mowat (retired), Shona Clark, Fiona MacLeod, Sandy Watson, Elizabeth Harris, Jean Greig, John Skinner, Liz Gourlay

Third row: Alex Fitzpatrick (retired), George Cockburn (retired), Robert Paton (Treasurer), Jimmy Brown, Ramsay Withycombe, Ronnie Sinclair, Tom Greig, David Arthur, Jim Milroy, Stewart Cairns

Fourth row: Jim Reid (retired), Marshall Wyllie, Ian Stubbs (Finance Convenor), Marianne MacGregor, Lindsay McKendrick, John Henderson, Stewart Drummond, Mervin Aiken, Jim McKerral, Jim Shaw, Campbell Scouler, Ian Hutchison, Arthur Croall

The Fabric Committee (page 116)
Roger Eason, Jim Shaw, Bobby Fullerton, John Henderson, Norman Anderson, Ramsay Withycombe, Walter Smyth
Committee members not pictured: Jim McKerral, Barbara Bremner, John Dawson, Arthur Croall, Bryan Robertson, Stewart Lothian

Finance Committee (page 116)
Left to right: Jimmy Brown, John Skinner, Robert Paton (Treasurer), Donald Fraser, Bill Jenkins, Liz Ronald, Ian Stubbs (Convenor)

Safeguarding Group (page 117)
Isobel Dawson, Stewart Drummond, Margaret Hamilton

Pastoral Group (page 117)
Left to right: Margaret Withycombe - Sandra McFarlane - Christine Murchie - Mary Deas – Anne Scott - Marion Mowat - Irene Frew - Rosemary Baillie - Jean Henderson (Leader) - Sandy Watson - Isabelle Dyer

Choir (page 118)
Front row – seated – from right to left:
Elspeth McDougall, Liz Ronald, Sheila Goldie, Alison Waterston, Grace Stevenson, Doreen Georgeson

Immediately behind seated row, from right to left: Jean Duffus, Irene McKerral, Isobel Dawson, Louise Macaulay, Doreen Green, Margaret West

Third row – from right to the far left: John Henderson, Sandy Watson, Arthur Gardner, Ian Murray, Jean Riddell, Jim McKerral, Stewart Cairns, Jean Henderson, Doris Watson (Organist & Choir Mistress).

Choir Performance of Stainer's Crucifixion (page 119)
Front row: right to left: Jean Duffus, Liz Ronald, Elspeth McDougall, Anne Sword, Christine Milleken, Margaret West, Louise Macaulay

Second row: right to left: Doris Watson, Piano & Choir Mistress, Marion MacDonald, Andrea Gibson, Lois McGinty, Irene McKerral, Jean Riddell, Jean Henderson, Sandra McKay, Doreen Green, Sheila Goldie

Third row: right to left: Jim McKerral, Ian Murray, Sandy Watson, Walter McGinty, John Mallan, Marje Gillies, Grace Stevenson

Last row, right to left: John Henderson, Roland Green, Arthur Gardner, Alan Mathew, Stewart Cairns, Isobel Dawson, Margaret Hamilton

Choir with organist Sandy MacPherson & Rev. Roderick Campbell (page 120)
Right to left: Front row: Rev. Roderick Campbell, Mary Ballantyne, Hilda Henderson, Elisabeth Martin, Sheila Clingan, Margaret West, Nancy Anderson, Nessie Hydes, Sandy MacPherson

Second row: left to right: May Taylor, Bette Thetford, Elspeth McDougall, Ann Mitchell, Ann McCance, Helen Young, Jessie Keith, Mary Adye
Third row: right to left: Graham Clingan, George Wilson, Andrew Walker, Hamish Grant, David Carstairs

Appendices - Bibliography

Choir – possibly at Easter 1984 (page 120)
Left to right: Front row: Margaret West, May Taylor, Bette Thetford, Nessie Hydes, Ann Mitchell, Helen Young
Second row: Name Unknown, Catherine Walker, Jessie Keith, Chris Milroy, Mary Ballantyne, Jean Laird
Third row: George Wilson, Organist Sandy MacPherson, Andrew Walker

Choir in 2008 with retiring organist Jean Binning (page 120)
Left to right: Front row: Doris Watson, Elspeth McDougall, Sandy Watson, Jean Binning, Liz Ronald, Sheila Goldie, Margaret West, Fiona Lyon

Second row: Alistair Wilson, Stewart Cairns, Jean Duffus, Norman Anderson, Doreen Georgeson, Jean Riddell, Grace Stevenson, Alison Waterston, Doreen Green, John Henderson

Woman's Guild (page 121)
Main group photo – taken at the AGM on 4th April 2012:
Front row seated – left to right:
Ina White, Louise Macaulay, Jessie Campbell, Barbara Aiken, Irene McKerral, Anne Scott, Betty Cruickshank, Janne Farnham, Nancy Anderson

Standing first row:
Jessie Fraser, Betty Stanage, Ian Watson, Ina Dodds, May Glaister, Jean Stairmand, Terry Docherty, Irene Stewart, Ella Skinner, Lorna Combs, Doris Watson, Rena Cuthbertson, Sheila Goldie, Evelyn Hume, Barbara Bennet

Standing second row:
Jean Britton, Betty Hall, Betty Carvel, Elizabeth Kay, Ann Reekie, Helen Telford, Marion Campbell, Margaret Grant, Jean Dunning, Maureen Aird, Wilma Mitchell, Marianne Deas, Margaret Aird, Marion McGee

The Woman's Guild Singers (page 122)
from left to right: Barbara Aiken, Jean Howie, Jean Laird, Bette Thetford, Nancy Anderson, Ina White, Fay Stevenson, Nessie Hydes, Maisie Beggs (Pianist)

Last performance in 1998 (page 122)
From left to right: Seated: Sheila Goldie, Nancy Anderson, Maisie Beggs, Ella Skinner; Standing: Barbara Aiken, Ina White, Ann Scott, Betty Mcinnes, Marion McGee

Appendices - Bibliography

Woman's Guild Singers & Performers On and Off Stage (page 123)
Close up off stage
from left to right: Bette Thetford, Jean Howie, Jean Stairmand, Ella Reid, Ina White, Barbara Aiken, Nessie Hydes

Centenary Cake cutting ceremony in 2011 (page 123)
Pictured from left to right: Jessie Fraser, Terry Docherty, Margaret McColl, Mary Lightfoot, Ina Watson – all ladies in their 90's. (Secretary Helen Telford standing behind the group)

Mission Group (page 124)
Left to right:
Susan Fraser, Violet Kavanagh, Elizabeth Harris, Tom Greig, Jean Greig, Irene McKerral, Kay Galloway and Jessie Joliffe

Friendship Singers (page 125)
Left to right: Doreen Green, Doreen Georgeson, Alison Waterston, Jean Riddell, Elspeth McDougall, Fiona Whitelaw, Rae Cairns, Jean Binning, Anne Sword, Isobel Dawson, Sheila Goldie, Christine Murchie, Jean Duffus

Friendship Club Committee (page 126)
From left to right: Front row – seated: Nancy Fisher, Jean Greig, Thelma Rockall, Isabelle Dyer, Eleanor Fullerton, Morag Dougan, Evelyn Hume, Pat Goodwin

Standing – row behind: Betty Hall, Louise Macaulay
Also on the Committee but not pictured: Maureen Andrews, Elspeth McDougall, Aileen Fyfe, Norma Anderson, Irene Frew

The Flower Committee (page 127)
From left to right: Jill Dickie, Betsy McKinlay, Rosemary Baillie, Ella Skinner, Margaret Withycombe, Jessie Campbell, Joan Stubbs

Appendices - Bibliography

Youth Club Planting Mission (page 128)
In the centre of the photo, Impact Team leader, Neil MacLennan holding a spade beside the oak tree sapling which is being planted.

In a circle around Neil, from left to right: Liz Gourlay, Unknown boy, Andrew Kimble (turned away), Pauline Maclean (now Mrs Colin Forster), Aileen MacLennan, Colin Forster, Rebecca, Stuart Douglas, Rev. Joe Kavanagh, Kenny Maddock (with Impact sweatshirt), Grant MacGregor, Scott Runciman, Fraser Collingham and Stephen Paul (with hood on), Jonathan McKinney and Ian Campbell.

Sunday Club with Moderator – February 2013 (page 129)
Front row:
Jamie Boyce, Harrison Jack, Richard Eagers-Hardie, Mrs Fiona MacLeod – Sunday Club Co-ordinator, Very Rev. Albert Bogle, Rebecca Boyd, Eilidh Fraser, Rev. Joe Kavanagh, Blair Fraser, Cameron Fraser,
Second row:
Lewis Telfer, Molly Telfer, Lorna MacDonald, Kirsty MacDonald, Erin Boyce, Elspeth McCalman, Grace Gilbride (with hat)

Back rows:
Mrs Liz Gourlay, Mrs Kate Telfer, Mrs Valerie Howie, Mrs Ann Richardson Boyce, Mrs Jill Jack, Mrs Claire Boyd, Mrs Barbara MacDonald, Fiona Smyth, Miriam Gilbride, Matthew MacLeod, Ian Campbell, Susan Howie, Mrs Audrey Gilbride, Holly Jack, Matthew Gilbride, Charlotte Clough

Junior Church Staff September 2012 (page 130)
Left to right: Liz Gourlay, Maria Farquhar, Fiona MacLeod (Sunday Club Co-ordinator), Emma Stevenson (Youth Worker), Margaret Paul (Assistant Co-ordinator), Heather Smyth, Barbara MacDonald

1st Mearns Guides (page 130)
Sofia Bald, Keira Campbell, Lucy Connelly, Emily Crusher, Amy Davis, Anna Gallagher, Hannah Garside, Iona Gibson, Lois Hanna, Lucy Holmes, Susan Howie, Emma Jeffrey, Elizabeth Kidd, Margaret Kidd, Elaine Kirk, Elspeth McCalman, Rhona McCalman, Kirstie Noble, Alix Paterson, Beth Paterson, Cara Pearson, Melissa Pearson, Holly Phillips, Lauren Quinn, Jessica Ramsay, Lauren Scott-Kiddie, Emma Stewart, Heather Stewart, Erin Wharton, Emma Watson, Kirsten Watson, Victoria Wight, Morna Weir

Appendices - Bibliography

Leaders:
Fiona Milne, Gemma Hanton, Kirsten Barclay, Rachael Gemmell, Kennedy Inglis, Victoria Motherwell

Mother and Toddlers Group (page 131)
From left to right
Susan Graham (in charge of tea & coffee for over 15 years), Abby, Becky and Avril Slack, Kerry & Charlie Sutton, Jenny-Lee & Rory Kely, Jane & Ellen Barbary, Susanne Bell & Max Hose, Denise & Gavin Fairlie, Laura & Gregor Hails, Cari, Ben & Katie Raleigh, Samantha & Heather Corrie, Anita & Maya Johnstone, Jennifer & Cameron Robertson, Julie & Kiera McKane, Elizabeth & Adam Tortolano, Lauretta & Finn Lavalette, Kirsty & Jessica Johnston, Belinda Perri & Oscar Mangiacasade, Liz & Olivia Deighton, Julie & Kirsty Pearson, Stephanie & Kirstin Syme, Laura, Nathan & Maisy Judge, Annabelle Landie & Joseph Cox, Sharon & Aimee Porter

Keep Fit Club (page 132)
Left to right:
Front row: Name unknown, Elspeth McDougall, Jean Binning, Evelyn Hume, Margaret West, Irene Knox, May Macintosh, Doreen Georgeson, Dorothy Walker, Fiona Whitelaw, Beryl Young, Mina Copeland

Second row:
Olive Jones, Joan McLean, Jean Patrick, Carole Ure, Margaret Morrison, Pat Goodwin, Amelia Egan, Val Buckberry, Maureen Andrews
Third row: Anne Scott, Jessie Brown, Janne Farnham, Alison Howarth, Nellie Laidlaw, Jean Riddell, June Stewart, Katie Grant, Ann McQuade

The Ladies Walking Club (page 133)
Jean Webb, Pat Carruth, Eleanor Aitken, Irene Graham, Harriet Reid, Celia Corbett, Anne McGhee

Mixed Badminton Club (page 134)
From the left to right: Front row: Heather Anderson, Penny Rowell, Trishaw McMorris, Irene Wyllie

Back row: John Rowell, Ken Mitchell, Maureen Mitchell, Lyn Black, William Black, Eric Morris

Bibliography

Electronic Sources

Register of Paisley Monastery 1163-1529, Via Glasgow University Library and TannerRitchie Publishing, Burlington Canada

Episcopal Register of Glasgow 1100-1560 Vol 1 via Glasgow University Library and TannerRitchie Publishing, Burlington Canada

Secondary sources
Journal Articles

'The Capelrig Cross' and 'Sculptured Slab at Kilmaronock' *Proceedings of The Society of Antiquaries of Scotland*, session mcmxxvi-mcmxxvii (January 10 1927) 139-142

Toolis, R., ' Bronze Age Pastoral Practices in the Clyde Valley, Excavations at West Acres Newton Mearns' *Proceedings of The Society of Antiquaries of Scotland*, 135 (2005) 471-504

Johnston, M., and Rees, A. 'Excavation of and Early Historic Palisaded Enclosure at Titwood, Mearnskirk, East Renfrewshire'. *Scottish Archaeological Journal*, Vol 25 (2002) 129-145

Books
Barr, James., *The Scottish Covenanters* (John Smith and Son, Glasgow, 1946)

Boyd Scott, Rev A, *Old days and Ways in Newton Mearns* (Pickering and Inglis, Glasgow, 1939)

Burleigh, J.H.S, *A church History of Scotland* (Oxford University Press; Oxford, 1960)

Dupuy, R.E., and Dupuy,T.N., *The Collins Encyclopaedia of Military History* 4th Edn, (Collins, Glasgow, 1993)
Henderson, G. and Henderson, I., *The Art of the Picts*, '*Sculpture and Metal work in early medieval Scotland*' (Thames and Hudson, London, 2011)

Appendices - Bibliography

Kenyon et al., T*he Civil Wars; A Military History of England Scotland and Ireland 1638-60* (Oxford University Press, Oxford, 1998)

Kidd, Lesley, with Loudon, Anne., *Mearns Matters*

Lumsden, John., *The Covenants of Scotland* (Gardiner; Paisley, 1914)

Metcalfe W.A., *A History of Paisley 600-1900* (Gardiner; Paisley, 1895)
[By e-book from the University of Toronto]
Moisley H.A et al., Third statistical account of Scotland (Collins, Glasgow, 1962)
Nicolaisen W, I, H. S*cottish Place Names* (new edition)(John Donald, Edinburgh, 2001)

Oliver, Neil., *A History of Scotland* (Phoenix Press, London ,2009)

Scott, H., *Fasti Ecclessiae Scoticanae,* Vol 3, Synod of Glasgow and Ayr

Sinclair, Sir John., New Statistical Account of Scotland, 1791-1799, Vol VII.

Walker, W.A, Twelve Centuries of Christian Witness, (Mearnskirk, 1982)

Watson, William, J, *The History of the Celtic place names of Scotland*, (Edinburgh 1926)

Watt, Hugh., *Recalling the Scottish Covenants* (Nelson Press, London, 1946)

Welsh T.C., *Eastwood District, History and Heritage* (Eastwood District Libraries, 1989)

Maps
All maps used in this publication were viewed online from the National Library of Scotland

Ainslie, J.,	1796, Map of the County of Renfrew
Blaeu, J.,	1654, 'Renfrewona'
Moll, H.,	1745, 'The Shire of Renfrew with Cunninghame'
Pont, T.,	1590, 'Renfrewshire'
Roy, W.,	1746-1755, 'Military Survey of Scotland'

Appendices - Bibliography

Thomson, J.,   1826, 'Renfrewshire'
Ordinance Survey first edition 1863 'Renfrewshire'

Newspapers
Glasgow Herald, *Sale of Land, Titwood of Mearns*, 12 July 1833 p5

Glasgow Herald, *Sale of Land, Davieland and Whitecraigs*, June 16 1856 p12

Glasgow Herald, *Old Mearns Parish Church Opening*, 15 March 1932 p5

Glasgow Herald, *Weathercock for Church Building*, 3 October 1945 p10

Websites
National Library of Scotland, http://www.nls.uk/

Royal Commission on Ancient and Historic monuments of Scotland (RCAHMS) www.rcahms.gov.uk/

Paradox of Medieval Scotland, http://www.poms.ac.uk/

My Armoury.com for Swords http://www.myarmoury.com/features.html